The
Business of
Security

and the

Security of
Business:

A Business Tale for Cyber Interaction

Contents

INTRODUCTION

This is NOT a security book in the classic sense. There are no in-depth details concerning specific tools, settings, configurations, or 'pure' security management. It doesn't delve into the standard Identify, Protect, Detect, Respond, and Recover aspects. The intent is not to train security professionals on security tools or processes, but rather to provide examples of business interaction as a guide to enable their ability to enhance the business. In turn, this will provide a common foundation for business leaders and hopefully spark critical thinking and a dialogue that is not adversarial.

What's the purpose of cybersecurity? In its simplest form, it's to protect businesses, public organizations, or assets from cyber harm; whether intentional or unintentional. This is a highly simplistic view, but not inaccurate.

This book elaborates on the part of cybersecurity that is frequently overlooked; the need to enhance and improve the business, both top and bottom lines. To do this, security professionals must understand the business intent and more of the business processes.

The examples in this book are about collaboration, understanding, and teamwork. The importance of those aspects

should not surprise anyone, yet it's one of the most difficult lessons to learn and execute.

There have been some noticeable and disturbing trends in the cyber security world that have stood out above the rest. Obviously, the significant rise in cybercrime/impact, driven by Nation State, Organized Crime, hacktivists, fraudsters, etc., is a key concern, as is the ever-increasing number of threats and vulnerabilities.

Another interesting factor has been the emergence and maturation of the malicious ecosystem, essentially creating a lucrative and sustainable business model for everything from phishing, ransomware development, DDoS as a service, to the multitude of other services that mirror the more conventional, 'law-abiding' market space.

We can also observe a gap on the defensive side. This is not referring to the tools or frameworks that have been developed, as there are some incredibly powerful tools, applications, and thought leadership in the security space. The gap is specifically in how well the security leaders, especially those that have come up purely through the security ranks, truly understand and collaborate well to enable and enhance the business. Executives, leaders, and academics alike have expressed concern with this issue. While there has been progress in this area, there is still a significant gap between the realities and perceptions of business

executives and their security counterparts. This book was written to help exemplify the issue and bridge the gap.

This book has been written as a fictional story but is intended to provide real-world meaningful insights. The story contains examples of how to effectively partner and communicate between cybersecurity and the various business silos in order to better meet the needs of the business. The end goal in the real world is to show a transformative path towards security becoming a business enabler, able to provide secure methodologies to protect company data and assets, as opposed to remaining a perceived business inhibitor.

Since cybersecurity in defense of a business is only as strong as the understanding business executives have, this book is also aimed at them. The current way business leaders think about ROI needs to be retooled when considering security to take into account both the soft and hard dollar implications. Security is as much about avoidance as it is about enablement, which makes discussions revolving around staffing and budgeting that much more difficult. These various factors need to be considered by executive leadership, which means they must have a rudimentary understanding of cybersecurity. We should not expect those business leaders to reach out or attend classes. It is the security leader's job to effectively communicate and provide valuable insights to the executive staff that is

not filled with Fear, Uncertainty, and Doubt (FUD).

You may think several items are 'missing' from the text or notice things that are different from industry to industry. This is to be expected. There are many nuances, facets, and complexities around cybersecurity, governance, risk, compliance, and general business decision-making processes. This is not intended to cover all eventualities. It is intended to be an example to make the reader think about their corollaries and the dynamics within their respective business or industry.

The characters' key learning experiences and evolution will guide security and business leaders to a common understanding and lexicon as well as progressive examples of risk definition and business case development. A hopeful outcome is that this book will assist cybersecurity managers/executives to grow professionally and evolve from a negative model, where the default response is "No", to one of support and enablement. As such, one of the primary themes of this book is the improvement of communication.

Many professionals in the cybersecurity field feel the necessity to protect a business from itself. While this is a commendable and admirable stance, in many instances it hinders the progression of business, and the core reason business is in place – to earn profit and increase margins. There needs to

be a common framework to allow security and the business to work in unison and jointly strive to meet the same goals. That way, security becomes a core function as to 'how' the business works.

Conversely, within that framework, business leadership grows and evolves to acknowledge security implications and comprehend the security requirements to allow for a slice of the budgetary pie. In this ever-changing cyber landscape, security is a requirement and no longer an afterthought. While many companies may outsource most of their cybersecurity needs, there is still an inherent cost and understanding that must come with it. For those that create 'in-house' security organizations, there are costs and additional implications that need to be understood and accepted.

The flow and format of this book is designed to tell a realistic story of a fictional regional financial institution in the Southeast. After solid growth, the company is expanding its market by acquiring a smaller financial firm in the Midwest. Through the story of the business acquisition and internal events, the characters face numerous challenges and interactions that they must professionally mature through to ensure business success.

The progression of the story will highlight the CISO as he goes through several events, which are now unfortunately common for most industries. In this process, the reader should be able to empathize, or at least

sympathize, with several of the scenarios. A notable item for some readers will be the early stages of the book and potentially cringeworthy scenarios. Others will follow the progression and hopefully have 'Ah-ha' moments that indicate an understanding of why the business leadership made certain decisions.

Security, specifically the vulnerabilities and threats it tries to protect businesses from, is constantly evolving. It is as nebulous and ephemeral as the hackers, fraudsters, malicious individuals, groups, organized crime, or nation states that are conducting the 'events'. Don't get hung up on the issue de jour, whether it's SIM Swapping, Phishing, Ransomware, DDoS, SQL Injection, or any of the hundreds of other potential issues. Threats, vulnerabilities, and protection will morph and change; the need for security to be part of the business does not.

Executive attention and approval on security requirements is more important than ever. The stakes are higher than ever. The general populace has heard more about cyberattacks and security in the last two years than in the last twenty. Security professionals need to understand the partnership with their business peers and collaborate to enhance and enable the business objectives.

This visibility comes with positive and negative implications that tend to create a pendulum swing rather than a grounding of intent and action. On one hand, the increased

visibility stimulates action on behalf of the business executives and board members. However, this creates a series of actions that are many times highly reactionary and not in alignment with the coherent roadmap the organizations should be driving towards. As a former boss and well-tenured CSO used to say frequently, "Never let a good crisis go to waste." Act quickly while the incident is still painful but ensure that the reaction is part of the overall roadmap.

A well-developed roadmap allows for action to be taken quickly, but without compromising strategic objectives. The preparation, planning, business inclusion, and action plans that can be developed in advance are critical and worthwhile investments. Roadmaps should be a core attribute that includes the business drivers as much as the common security frameworks in order to lead towards business enablement.

As you read the fictional story, consider the following: "What does business enablement mean and how does it relate to cybersecurity, which is often seen as a cost center?" Simply put, business enablement is "the creation of processes, tools, or actions that do not hinder business development, but rather enable a supportive and collaborative working exchange to further the core business."

This may be as simple as meeting with business owners to understand the thought

process behind specific decisions and collaborating with teams (IT or otherwise) to provide supportable, secure methods of conducting cyber-related transactions that are potentially outside the norm. This can be a door opener to find ways to securely meet business needs early in the definition process, rather than at the end stage of a critical project. While this method often places security teams outside of their comfort zone, it also ignites new thought processes and builds rapport between organizations.

Consider the advantage of being involved in the business requirement review process at the beginning of a major project, rather than as an afterthought (or worse – being left out due to being an inhibitor). Then consider the potential to build and support new methodologies and security technologies that improve the business that is being secured. Now consider why security has been left out at the earlier stages of the process.

As you watch the progression of the security leadership and the senior executive interactions within this book, reflect on interactions with subordinates, peers, and executives and how the evolution of the security maturation parallels the technology maturation just a few short years ago.

In 2011, David Rosenbaum wrote an article for *CFO Magazine* highlighting the challenges in the CIO/CFO interaction. It is remarkable

to see the growth and evolution that has taken place in that relationship. As the CIO/CFO interaction, and more importantly, the CIO/business interaction was noted at that time, the evolution to a common set of objectives and delivery of financial awareness has created a more rounded and business-focused CIO. A similar maturation must take place between security and the executive leadership. Business is more dependent on technology than ever, and technology is unfortunately subject to myriads of attack and fraud at an alarming pace from anywhere in the world.

As you read this book, remember why it was written. It is not designed to tell you how to run the technical aspects of your security department. Rather, it tells you the story of what is possible when security fully integrates with the rest of the business needs and begins to embrace its role.

Prologue

If the sound of the phone vibrating incessantly on top of the wooden nightstand hadn't woken Paul, the blinking light certainly would have done the trick. He couldn't believe how something so small could create such a blindingly white light. Groaning, he rolled over in bed and groggily swatted at the offending phone, attempting to shut it up before his wife woke up. He squinted to make out the blurry outline of the clock across the room as he brought the phone up to his ear.

1:57? There was never any good news this late at night.

"Yeah?" he grumbled, aware that he probably sounded half asleep.

"Boss, I've got some bad news. We're probably going to be on the news in the morning." The voice on the other end of the line was one he was very familiar with. Lisa, his Security Operations Center (SOC) Director, was one of his best managers – and one of the most frustrating. Still, her cryptic message had its intended effect and he found himself waking up rapidly, waiting for her to elaborate.

"Our fraud detection systems identified irregular behavior happening in our CRM databases. It looks like all our client and business intelligence data was downloaded and someone attempted to transfer it offsite."

Paul found himself pinching the bridge of his nose, the implications of what he was hearing racing through his mind.

"Hold on a second," he whispered into the phone.

Glancing over his shoulder to make sure he wasn't disturbing his wife, he slid out of bed, clicking on his nightstand light just long enough to find his glasses before turning it back off and making his way out of the room.

Still trying to wrap his mind around what he had been told, he started firing off a barrage of questions as he made his way down the stairs.

"Has a working bridge been opened? What is the Threat Detection team seeing? Have we confirmed this with the partner systems in Data? What's the scope of the loss? Have any authorities been involved yet? Have we locked down our outbound traffic? Is this due to an APT or is an active user doing this?"

There was an audible pause on the other end of the line before she started, "We don't know any of that yet – we just found out about this and I called you immediately, but…."

Paul cut her off, realizing she knew just as little as he did and was trying to tap-dance around the issue, "Yeah, I get that, thanks for letting me know. Let's get the Incident Response Team activated on this now. Get a working bridge going and start getting resources on site for review."

Within minutes the Incident Response Team (IR team) had established a bridge and Paul found himself pacing back and forth in his basement, monitoring the progress. After thirty minutes on the phone, the team had successfully contained the necessary systems and moved on to attempting to identify the scope of the data loss as well as possible ingress and egress routes that had been used. Paul listened as his leaders began assigning teams various responsibilities in order to cover down on a checklist of probable causes. After fielding a few clarifying questions, he dropped from the call by saying that he would be monitoring operations from the office and should be in in less than an hour.

Heading back to the bedroom to get dressed, he paused just long enough to bend over and kiss his wife on the forehead, whispering, "Happy anniversary," in her ear before sneaking out of the room.

Before backing out of the garage, he blasted off a quick message to the company's senior leadership. He included a quick summary of what he knew and promised to keep relevant parties informed as needed throughout the rest of the situation. His drive to work was relatively

uneventful, broken up only by the periodic chiming of his phone as updates from his teams were forwarded. Pulling into his typical parking spot, he was pleased to see cars belonging to his senior managers littered throughout the lot. The lights on the third floor were already on, indicating that the incident response team was in the building and digging into the data that was available to them.

Jim, the nighttime security guard at the front door, simply nodded as Paul walked in, no doubt expecting his presence given the alarming number of individuals that were pouring into the building at three in the morning. Paul opted to take the stairs, still working on his first cup of coffee, rather than wait for the archaic elevator to arrive and then slowly work its way up the forty-foot climb to the third floor.

It was a scene of controlled chaos as he opened the stairwell door, with his managers shouting over cubicles, trying to control their teams and maintain situational awareness of what the other teams were doing. Walking down the hallway, he caught Lisa's eyes over one of the cubicles and pointed towards his office. She nodded in understanding and turned to give a final piece of guidance to one of her staff before falling in step behind him.

Closing the door behind her, Lisa placed some preliminary reports on his desk and took a seat, waiting silently as he sifted through the papers she had handed him. He hoped he wasn't reading them correctly, but the more he read, the more he felt the cold sense of dread creeping through him.

"How did this happen?" he finally managed to say, putting the paperwork down in front of him and subconsciously pushing it as far away from him as possible.

"The best we can tell right now is that it was a flaw in the permissions for the temporary systems. Working with IT and the key business units, we placed all our data there to consolidate it properly before combining it with the new CRM systems. It was supposed to be a temporary thing, not a permanent solution, but we got delayed for a few days due to other

17

pressing issues. It got hit earlier this evening through some backdoor and the data started slowly being downloaded to an offsite location. The only reason we caught it is that whoever was on the other side got impatient towards the end and used up enough bandwidth to trigger some of our detection systems."

"Based on initial data, it looks like it had to have been an insider. With the existing security, there are at least two separate parties that would have to be involved in collusion for this to have happened. They appear to have been focused on PII & PCI data but were only able to get a minimal amount of data exfiltrated. We had deliberately segregated distinct PCI data elements to not allow for this in our primary systems. Unfortunately, we did not enable data masking, multi-factor authentication, or integrate full fraud detection systems that we would normally have in place since this was viewed as a quick transitory process. We did have 256-bit encryption set up in transit and at rest and required username and password setup for the access, but the entitlements were not at the same granular level we would normally adhere to. We've closed off access to the systems and have started compiling a full scope of the loss. What we don't know yet is if they dropped anything into our network or systems on their way out. There are a lot of unknowns at this time." She continued with a slightly uplifted tone, "but what we do absolutely know is what accounts were used internally and who was on the network during the breach. We can nail these bastards!"

Paul found himself pinching the bridge of his nose for the second time that night, squeezing his eyes shut as his mind raced furiously. "I thought we had planned for this," he said, feeling his temper rise. "Also, why wasn't I told that the data transitions were delayed? I thought I made it explicitly clear that any inconsistencies with the acquisition were to be brought to my attention, no matter how small an issue they appeared."

Getting even more agitated, he continued, "This wasn't even our responsibility! We volunteered to help alleviate the load on the IT team and now we've dropped the ball! Not only did we drop the ball, but we did it by failing to follow basic security principles... as the damn security

staff! Knowing who was on the network during the breach is good, but it doesn't fix the fact that it happened in the first place!"

"We didn't think much of the delay," Lisa replied, speaking slowly and clearly choosing her words carefully. "There were some unforeseen complications revolving around how some of the users and partner networks would access it, but it wasn't anything we weren't confident we could fix." She added the next piece carefully, "And we made sure that we included the business and IT in every step since they technically own all the data and business processes."

Paul slammed his hand down on his desk, letting his emotions get the best of him as he looked up at Lisa. "I don't care whether you thought you could fix it or not! Or who was involved! My guidance was explicit. There was no room for misunderstanding. And yet, here I am, being blindsided by a breach that will be pasted across the front page of every newspaper later today!"

"I don't know what to say, boss. I screwed up, but my team is working frantically right now to try and fix the issue."

Paul sighed loudly, trying to calm himself down as he began thinking ahead towards what needed to be done. "Alright," he said after a long pause, "keep your team working on it. I want a status update in an hour so I have some more information to arm myself with. Right now, I want all the systems housing this information taken off the network. We should be able to manually handle it for the next few hours until the East Coast starts waking up. At that point we'll have to go back online, but at least we have a few hours to breathe."

Lisa nodded and quietly stood up, excusing herself from his office and walking quickly back to her team's working area. Paul watched her for a bit before reaching out and pulling the reports back across his desk towards him. Lisa meant well, but they would never be able to recover the data. It was too far gone at this point. The next step was to understand what was lost and to make sure it didn't happen again. One

way or another, he knew before long that he would have to answer for what had happened.

Skimming through the report one more time to make sure he had his facts straight, Paul reached across his desk and grabbed his phone. Punching in the numbers from memory, he listened as the phone started ringing. Finally, after the fourth ring, he was rewarded by a click followed by a tired voice, "Hello...?"

Taking a deep breath, Paul leaned forward in his chair and began, "Brandon. We've confirmed the issue..."

PART ONE

Chapter 1

Nine months earlier

Monday, 9 January

"Look, all I'm saying is that I think we've solidified our standings in the Southeast enough to begin pursuing expansion elsewhere. The Midwest is ideal for us, given what our analysts are saying, and I think this firm in particular has some great growth opportunities that we can help guide and shape."

"We completely understand your point, Brandon, and wholeheartedly endorse the idea of expansion. We are just trying to ensure that you understand some of the inherent risks involved and have planned accordingly. Transitioning from being a regional institution to a national one is a fairly decisive move, and it has the potential to create backlash amongst some of your stauncher supporters, who will more than likely feel that you are moving towards a less personal interaction approach as opposed to the more bespoke service they currently have with Windward Financial Group; which is why you've been so successful."

Brandon eyed Tom from across the table, trying to figure out how to proceed. Tom had been Chairman of the Board when Brandon was brought on as CEO and had always had a habit of voicing his opinion without outright giving guidance. On one hand, this had allowed Brandon to experiment with some unique business ideas during his tenure as CEO, but on the other hand, instances like this made it a pain.

"You'll have to excuse me," Brandon said, speaking deliberately, "but I'm having a hard time understanding if you support this deal moving forward or if your reservations are keeping you from endorsing it."

Tom leaned forward, resting his elbows on the table, and studied Brandon for an uncomfortable moment as though deciding how to best respond. Finally, he said, "Perhaps a bit of both. The growth potential you've outlined is fantastic and definitely stands on its own when validating this move. From what we've seen in our private discussions, the business goals line up perfectly. However, going public with this means that there will be no easy way to turn back. The proverbial die will be cast. Everyone in this room agrees that it makes sense. It's just a timing concern at this point."

"What more do you need to see for me to convince you that this is the appropriate time to go forward with this?" Brandon asked, taking note that all the other board members in the room had nodded in agreement with Tom's remarks.

"Marketing strategy," Jerry, the board member sitting directly to Brandon's right, cut in, pausing just long enough to receive a silent nod from Tom before continuing. "Not marketing a specific product per se, but rather, how you plan to market this deal to investors and customers. Everyone in this room has been privy to the ups and downs of these discussions so far. It has been a long process, but ultimately, we have arrived at the point where we all agree that this acquisition is the right deal. Our customers won't give us as much time to convince them. Either they'll be onboard with the initial public release, or they won't be. It will be very hard to win them back over after that point."

"We've had organizational restructuring before," Brandon said, turning in his chair and facing Jerry directly. "In all past cases, it has been about being open and honest and identifying the risks but also highlighting the potential gains for our customers and investors. In this case, I think those gains will be self-evident."

"Yes," Tom said from his side of the table, "but in this case you will be merging two separate organizations. A complete process and infrastructure change will be occurring simultaneously while you are trying to expand your mission and scope. Employment requirements will

fluctuate, noncritical redundancy will have to be managed and eliminated, and you will be merging two disparate networks and attempting to reconcile and converge existing architecture. Nobody in this room is saying it can't be done. Clearly, we believe it can since we have gotten this far. Instead, what we are asking is whether you have the appropriate information and confidence to convince everyone else that this can be done."

Jerry nodded vigorously to Brandon's right, punctuating Tom's key point by wrapping his knuckles on top of the table.

"Additionally," Tom continued, "there is always the issue of information integration. One of the first things we'll want to do shortly after we close is merge our customer information with theirs. This will extend our current offerings and enable us to start with your proposed national service. This ultimately will require heavy lifting by your IT department. That by no means is a reason not to do this, but before we move forward with making this deal public knowledge I would at least like some initial feedback to ensure we won't be caught off guard when the IT infrastructure fails to handle this appropriately."

Brandon leaned over and pulled the manila folder that he had brought with him from under his chair, reaching inside and selecting the top sheet, before sliding it across the table to Tom. "I've already had some preliminary reports drafted up by Russell with regards to what sort of strain, if any, this would put on our IT systems. Based on early discussions with Pacific Group Finance facilitated by a third-party law firm, he has been able to draft up a sketch of their network and how they've handled data, application, and systems. He has assured me that the move won't be overly stressful. There will be some kinks to work out at first, yes, but in the grand scheme of things he feels that the IT aspect of the acquisition will be only a minor speed bump. As for the public perception," Brandon said, pushing a second sheet of paper across the table, "we've done some brainstorming in our PR and marketing departments. This is a list of the proposed ways to spin the risks while highlighting the potential gains, just as you mentioned. I've also got an additional list of items here that

outlines some of the smaller foreseeable challenges, such as market differences, state legislation issues, as well as key leadership merging."

Brandon was rewarded for his comments with silence as everyone in the room stared at either him or Tom. Suddenly Tom broke out laughing, slamming his fist on the table, and shaking with mirth in an uncharacteristic display of emotion. "I'll be damned! Here I was thinking this was going to be a long drawn-out experience and you've gone and proved again why we picked you to lead this company. This is fantastic," he said, spreading the documentation out in front of him. "So what you're telling me is you've already done a complete analysis, both internal and external, and you still believe this is the best move?"

"Absolutely. Look, I know there's some concern on the board about possible impacts to our momentum. We've had a tremendous few quarters, and Wall Street currently has us pegged to exceed the 8% growth we initially promised them this year. I care just as much about beating that goal as everyone else in this room, and I openly admit that this plan has a few inherent risks, but the growth opportunity is simply too good to pass up in my eyes."

"I think everyone in this room agrees with that last point," Tom said, still smiling but far more in control, "and I think given what you've provided us with, I speak for the board when I say that we should definitely move forward with your proposal."

Brandon saw heads going up and down in unison out of the corners of his eyes as he continued to meet Tom's gaze.

"Now," Tom continued, "unless anyone else has any major issues to bring up, I think we're done here. Anyone?"

Pausing a few moments to allow anyone the opportunity to speak up, Tom finally said, "Well then, I think that's that. Brandon, I assume you understand that we will be expecting a more detailed strategy shortly. For now, what you've provided will do. But from what you said at the

beginning, this has the potential to happen very rapidly, and I'd like to be prepared."

Brandon looked around the table and nodded to everyone. "No issues. I'll bring this up at my standing leadership meeting on Thursday and will get everyone working on it. I don't think it will take very long to have a clear idea of what will be required."

Brandon slid his chair back and stood up, smoothing the front of his suit jacket as he watched everyone else in the room gather up their belongings. Board meetings were always hit or miss, but this one had gone about as well as he could have expected. Tom had a history of being extremely demanding at the start of larger initiatives and then slowly losing interest and fading into the background as soon as they built up speed. This was admittedly the largest undertaking the company had done since its inception, but Brandon was still confident that once he got the ball rolling on this, the stress from the board would rapidly diminish.

Jerry patted him on the back, jarring him from his thoughts. "Well done, Brandon. I wanted to let you know that we didn't intend to blindside you, we just all wanted to make sure that the decision was being made with all possible variables considered. From the looks of it, you've done a phenomenal job of doing your homework and have the confidence of the board. I have no doubt this acquisition will go off without a hitch, in no small part because of the work you've done."

Brandon expressed his appreciation for the support and excused himself from the room before he could get wrapped up in any other small talk. Pulling his cell phone out of his pocket, he walked briskly towards the exit, nodding to Stacy, his CFO, on the way out to indicate that he was leaving.

"Matt," he said, lifting his phone up to his ear to speak to his COO. "The board approved the plan and we'll be going public with it. Go ahead and put out that Thursday's weekly meeting will probably run a bit longer than usual. Stacy is going to draft up some numbers for us between now

25

and then so that we can go ahead and get a start on some of the financial impacts."

After answering some of Matt's questions, Brandon clicked his phone off and tossed it in the center console of his car before pulling out, excited to get back to the office and finally go public on this project that had been so long in the making.

Chapter 2

Thursday, 12 January

Paul wrote furiously in his notebook as Brandon continued speaking, elaborating on how the deal would proceed. Everyone in the company had heard the rumblings about the possibility of moving forward with an acquisition, but Paul had still been surprised when he sat down in the weekly meeting only to immediately hear about the board approval and going public with the announcement of the acquisition of Pacific Group Finance. Lisa was seated next to Paul, writing just as furiously in her own notebook. She had been a great asset over the last eight months as Paul had gotten settled into his job as the Chief Information Security Officer (CISO) for Windward Financial Group. Her background was a little unorthodox, as she had spent all her career up until she came to WFG two years ago in the government, working on various security issues of national importance.

Evidently the bureaucracy had gotten to her, or so she said, because she'd made the transition to the civilian sector under the previous CISO. She still carried a few traits from her government experience, the most obvious of which was her absolutely unshakable belief that everything that could be secured should be, but she was exceptionally good at what she did.

Paul for his part was feeling a bit overwhelmed by what he was hearing. He had been on the staff overseeing an acquisition before, having spent the previous nineteen years of his career at various stages in the entertainment industry. Still, he had never been at the top of the security pyramid and had always had someone else above him to default to, should he need some guidance. This was his show now. The entire company would be looking at him and his staff to make the security decisions for the acquisition, as well as continue to secure the current systems, which was already a massive struggle given budgetary restrictions.

The security architecture he had inherited from his predecessor left a lot to be desired. There hadn't seemed to be a strategy, and instead various security measures had been placed haphazardly to cover up or deflect problems. The staff had been in a constant state of reactive panic, and it had taken all his focus until now to get them onto a more proactive footing. There was still a lot that needed to be done, however, and an acquisition certainly wasn't going to make any of it easier.

Lisa apparently shared some of his worries because she continued to shake her head slightly from side to side as she underlined key points on her notepad with a vengeance while listening to Brandon's strategy. Finally, after over an hour of speaking and diagramming various ideas on the whiteboard, Brandon apparently lost his steam and trailed off, opening it up to questions in the room.

Mitch, as usual, was the first one to open his mouth. He managed the most profitable team that oversaw the small and midsize business (SMB) client care program for WFG, which had done a phenomenal job at generating revenue, and more importantly, customer retention, over the past few years. As such, Mitch tended to have a high view of his opinions and took whatever opportunity he could to speak. He was great at what he did, if not a bit full of himself because of it.

"What do you perceive as the way ahead for the care of the business customer base? Obviously, we can't just let that product or our service offerings fall by the wayside, since it's producing the biggest cash flow for us. My recommendation would be to develop a standing cell that is ready to conduct the same sort of business management for the new territory we would be operating in. My current staff is too small to handle the doubled customer base efficiently, but with a few more bodies and more money to put into our data analytics programs I see no reason why we can't be just as successful, if not more successful, in the new region."

Brandon stood up and drew another diagram on the white board, depicting one circle over the top of two other circles. In the top circle, he

wrote "Mitch", while in the bottom two he wrote SE and MW, obviously meaning Southeast and Midwest.

"You're exactly right, Mitch. We can't afford to let our most profitable department suffer, or 'fall by the wayside' as you put it, especially considering it's what we are best known for. At the end of the day, this is a business move designed to enter a new market, generate market growth, and increase revenue and profitability. I've talked to Stacy about the way ahead with the budget and we both agreed that the safest bet would be to invest money according to the historical ROI each business sector offers us. Now is not the time to be guessing or trying to predict what will produce the best future ROI. Instead, we will rely on past numbers to get us through this transition safely. In that regard, your staff will be given additional funding to help enable you to establish your second team. I would ask, however, that you investigate Pacific Group Finance for talent before looking externally."

Mitch nodded, eyeballing the diagram on the board, apparently pleased with where and how his name was displayed. Paul did some quick mental math and was able to guesstimate that Mitch's organization would grow by no less than 40% in order to make a second team capable of matching the one he currently ran in the Southeast. The budget increase that would take was a little mind-boggling, but then again, so too were the numbers being proposed for the growth potential with this deal. Paul wondered how he did it. Mitch seemed to consistently have Brandon's favor and was often getting both accolades, and more importantly, financing for the projects he undertook. While Paul continually felt understaffed and underappreciated, Mitch appeared to have neither of those issues. Paul liked Mitch on a personal level, so he never felt any hostility towards Mitch, just a small pang of jealousy at how easy it was for Mitch to navigate the inner workings of the company. Lost in his thoughts, Paul didn't realize he was still staring until he saw Mitch shoot him a wink from across the room. Shaking his head to clear his thoughts, Paul smiled briefly in return before turning his attention back towards the head of the table.

Stacy spoke next, addressing the room as opposed to Brandon. "From a finance perspective, I feel that I need to underscore what Brandon just said. Now is not the time for us to be taking risks or making unnecessary expenditures. Sticking with what we know works is the easiest way to make this acquisition as painless as possible. As soon as everything is done, then we can start looking at more long-term investments. For the present, though, I would ask that all budgetary requests be viewed through the lens of whether it's an established item or not."

Paul could hear Lisa's pen still working overtime on her notepad and couldn't resist glancing down to see what she was working on. In big, bold lettering she had filled up an entire page with the word *HOW* and was busy adding multiple question marks all around the paper, apparently reacting to what Stacy had just said.

After a few other questions pertaining to various aspects of the deal, each dealing with a department outside of IT, there was finally a lull in conversation long enough for Paul to interject.

"I don't want to be the one who becomes known as doom and gloom, but I just wanted to bring it to everyone's attention that this has the potential to be a security nightmare. I appreciate Stacy's stance, it will certainly make it easier to not have to worry about anything new outside of this acquisition, but the security considerations will still be significant. At the very least, I'll need an increase in budget just to allow for the analysis to figure out the manpower and work hours that will most likely be required. Most of our competitors are supporting their security units with 5-6% of the overall IT budget. Last time I ran the numbers, my staff is limping away with barely 1.5%. Unless that number comes up, we run the risk of not being able to keep up with the threats."

"Paul, we appreciate your candid feedback; this is definitely the venue in which to voice it. However, Russell has already done a lot of the analysis you mentioned and has assured me that there should be no major flaws as a result of this deal," Brandon replied.

Paul had to keep himself from gaping at Russell, the CIO, across the room. When had that analysis been done? Paul's staff certainly hadn't been consulted on the issue when deciding whether or not there would be vulnerabilities. Still, that was certainly not something Paul was going to say here. Not in front of everyone.

"Besides," Brandon continued, apparently oblivious to Paul's confused glances at the CIO, "as Stacy mentioned, we are trying to limit investments in items that don't provide us with a firm, established ROI."

Paul winced as he saw Lisa open her mouth, knowing that whatever she was about to say would be true, but also not well received. "Your ROI is the safety of your valuable information. If a breach occurs, then you could lose everything. I'd say that's worth something."

Brandon's eyes narrowed a bit as he turned his attention to Lisa, agitatedly fiddling with his pen cap while clearly struggling to maintain his smile.

"Be that as it may, Lisa, I feel that Paul and the rest of your staff have done a phenomenal job to date making sure we were secured against all threats. Why, just the other day Paul presented me with a chart that showed how simple changes in the focus and structure of your organization had allowed for far more effective monitoring and performance without costing a single penny. If you're capable of that, I have no doubt that your team is more than able to handle this challenge. Russell, do you still stand by the assessment you provided me?"

"Absolutely," Russell said, meeting Paul's gaze. "I am certain that my staff can merge the two infrastructures with no increase in threat surface and no introduction of vulnerabilities. I will continue to work closely with Paul and his staff on the matter and we will keep you informed of any changes to that assessment. For now, however, it stands."

"Perfect! What else do you all have?" Brandon asked, looking around the room, apparently done with Paul and Lisa's line of questioning. Paul caught Lisa glancing at him and gave her a slight shake of the head. It

wasn't worth the fight right now; not until he had had a chance to get to the bottom of this with Russell.

A few more individuals asked questions, but shortly thereafter the meeting reached an end, and everyone stood up to leave. Paul sent Lisa back to their section to begin briefing some of his other managers, while he stayed seated and waited for Russell to finish speaking with Mitch. As soon as he saw them split apart, Paul stood up and made a beeline across the room, intersecting Russell on the way to the door and falling in beside him.

Russell glanced sideways at him and kept walking, starting to speak before Paul got a chance. "Look Paul, I know what this is about. I'm sorry you didn't see the report I sent Brandon, which was an oversight on my end. It really didn't need much of your input, though. My guys are going to be doing the heavy lifting here, making sure all the systems can operate in the new environment. It shouldn't be a big deal for you guys, though. If we're secure, and Pacific Group Finance is secure, then we should be good, right?"

"Not really, Russell. Look, I'm not concerned that this deal is going forward. It sounds like a great business opportunity. My issue is being told that there was an analysis already done on the security requirements, which neither my staff nor I had any part in. M&As require a good deal of security planning, and I haven't even had a chance to sit down and think about this yet. Merging the identity and access management systems both internally and externally is going to be a huge undertaking. This will also require policy updates and patch version control throughout the entire process as well as a litany of other items that could bite us in the ass. This is going to be a lot more involved for my staff than you're making it sound, and from what I just heard, I'll be doing it on a shoestring budget. I'm not comfortable with any of this at all, and Lisa is about ready to lose her mind. You and I need to get on the same page and reopen this conversation with Brandon. Mark my words, if we push forward with this without a clear security strategy, it could be extremely problematic."

Russell nodded thoughtfully at that, although at the pace he was walking it seemed as though he wanted nothing more than to get back to his office and away from the conversation. "Alright, here's how we can do it then. I'm holding an internal meeting tomorrow, before the weekend, to talk with my staff about the way ahead. How about you, Lisa, and whoever else you want to bring, come to the meeting and we can approach it from both perspectives. After that, we can both go and talk with Brandon about what was decided and get his approval."

Less than 24 hours? That was very little time to do the analysis that would be required to take a firm stance. Still, Russell was throwing him a bone, even if it was a small one, and Paul found himself agreeing to attend the meeting before turning around to rush back to his section. This would likely take all evening, and as Paul began to think through the logistics of what would be required to prepare for the meeting in the morning, he began to draft up a mental checklist of tasks and who on his team would be best positioned to complete them.

He was so preoccupied with his mental gymnastics that he almost ran headfirst into Mitch as he rounded the corner next to the conference room he had just left a few minutes prior.

"Hey Paul, fancy seeing you rushing around like the world is burning down around you. Everything good in paradise?" Mitch said, grinning and clearly enjoying his own joke.

"Oh, you know, just making sure we don't run headfirst into a disaster. Same as usual," Paul replied, not bothering to stop, and instead skirting around Mitch and continuing his quick pace back towards his staff.

"Well, you know where to find me if you ever need help," Mitch said.

"Will do," Paul shot over his shoulder, wondering what Mitch possibly thought he could help with. It didn't really matter right now, whatever it was, and by the time Paul got back to his office he had all but forgotten about his encounter with Mitch.

Chapter 3

Friday, 13 January

Russell absentmindedly flipped through the two stacks of papers that had been laid on his desk that morning by Charlotte, one of his directors. The left stack he was intimately familiar with, an outline of all the processes and systems that his team at WFG was responsible for. The right stack was far less detailed and was his team's first attempt at doing the same sort of analysis for PGF's systems. All in all, he was confident that he would be able to deliver on all his promises to Brandon. There would be a good bit of work involved, but nothing in the packet before him raised any red flags.

Today's meeting was intended to double-check the work and to begin merging the two stacks, figuring out where the potential struggles would be and what could be done to avoid or mitigate them. The meeting wasn't scheduled to begin for another ten minutes, so he was still sitting in his office rereading the reports and responding to a few minor emails. He could see the entrance to the conference room from his desk and had seen Charlotte walk in a few moments prior to set the room up. He hadn't seen anyone else walk into the room yet. If he had one complaint with his team, it was that they were notorious for showing up mere moments before meetings were scheduled to begin. Still, he felt that if that was his only complaint with his team, then things were going well, all things considered.

Across the building, barely visible above the cubicles, Russell saw two heads coming around the corner from another section of the building. The taller one was clearly Paul, and Russell could only guess that the ponytail bobbing beside him belonged to Lisa. Despite himself, he found himself drumming his fingers on his desk and feeling his stress level rise just a bit. It wasn't that he disliked either Paul or Lisa, he actually quite liked both of them on a personal level. It was the fact that they constantly tried to slow down his processes, claiming they were trying to defend the

company against some never-before-seen threat that sounded like something straight out of a government conspiracy theory or science fiction novel. Amongst his crew they were often bitched about in closed-door meetings.

Paul rounded the far corner and Russell could see for the first time that he was carrying a large stack of papers, easily dwarfing the two stacks that Russell had on his own desk. Paul looked up and saw Russell watching him through the glass, nodding in recognition before both he and Lisa turned and walked into the conference room. Russell sighed and hit send on his last email, collecting the papers on his desk and making his way out of his office. There was no sense in leaving the two of them there alone with Charlotte while he sat in his office staring at the clock.

Paul and Lisa had already taken their seats by the time he arrived. Thankfully, they had sat along the wall as opposed to at the table in the center. More alarmingly, they were both hunched over the papers Russell had seen in Paul's hands and were talking in hushed tones about whatever was written. Charlotte was still in the room as well, lining up chairs on the opposite side of the room for all the managers and other attendees who wouldn't be sitting at the table. Russell stood awkwardly in the door for a few moments before clearing his throat and walking into the room.

Over the course of the next few minutes, the room filled up with the rest of his staff, taking their seats while Russell walked around and briefly spoke with various people. Paul and Lisa had gone back to studying their papers after shaking Russell's hand, but as the room filled up, he noticed that they were slowly putting their documentation away beneath their seats and beginning to speak with the people sitting near them.

Russell finally made his way to the front of the room and glanced at Charlotte, who nodded to confirm that all the attendees had arrived. Raising his hands a bit to quiet the room, Russell placed the two stacks of paper down in front of him and began speaking.

"As most of you should know by now, whether through formal channels or word of mouth, the acquisition of Pacific Group Finance was approved to go public this week by the board. We're here today to begin planning for the eventual merging of systems and to set up a rough outline of the IT timeline in support of the overall business move. We've got some representatives from our cybersecurity organization," he said, gesturing towards Paul and Lisa, "who will help keep us in check and ensure we don't create too many unnecessary vulnerabilities."

Pausing to take a breath, Russell cringed when he heard Paul's voice chime in, "Thanks for involving us in this. We don't want to be a pain or disrupt anything; we just want to make sure things are done as securely as possible."

Russell waited to make sure Paul was finished speaking before forcing himself to smile widely and acknowledge the comments, "Glad you could make it, Paul. We're looking forward to the insight your team can offer."

After a few more opening comments, Russell turned the meeting over to Charlotte, who began walking everyone through the two stacks of paper and the proposed workflow that her team had come up with. There was some lively back and forth between some of the managers, and slowly, over the course of two hours, his team began to develop a timeline for how the new systems would be integrated with the existing architecture. Charlotte did a fantastic job of keeping everyone on track, and after a while Russell found the discussion coming to an end as final guidance to various managers was issued.

Russell stood up once more at the head of the table and waited for the room to quiet. "Great work, everyone. I think everyone in this room should have a fairly solid idea of what's expected of them. I'll work with Charlotte to get more of these meetings on the calendar so that we can continue to sync our efforts. For now, though, unless anyone has anything else, I think we can call it here."

"Actually," Paul said, standing up and addressing the room from near the wall, "I was wondering if I could have a few moments to add my staff's

input into what was discussed today. I didn't want to continually interrupt as you all were brainstorming and problem-solving, but I think it's important to discuss the security implications of what was decided today before anyone goes out and starts making the changes."

Will, another one of Russell's directors, raised his hand from the seat of the table and interjected, "I don't think anything decided today should have too drastic a security concern to be quite frank. All we've decided today is how to configure certain systems to be able to accept data from PGF, which are already secure. Essentially, we are connecting two secure networks in order to make one. Nothing from the outside is coming in, so it should just be a matter of making sure we don't get rid of any of the security measures along the way."

Paul nodded thoughtfully during Will's comments, betraying no emotion as far as Russell could tell. "That would be absolutely correct, assuming we were 100% secure and so were they," Paul finally said after Will had stopped, "but it would be foolish to assume either of those things. Security is inherently flawed, and what you just mentioned highlights that fact, although not in the way you intended. We are essentially taking two networks and making them one, just as you said. However, each of those networks brings with them vulnerabilities, and we can't honestly say what will happen when those vulnerabilities stack on top of one another. My staff knows what our deficiencies are, or at least where to look for them, but we can't say the same for PGF."

Paul was slowly edging his way to the front of the room as he spoke, getting closer to Russell's seat as he continued talking. "My team looked at the systems PGF has, much like you did, but what we found were possible issues. They are using some software and data management systems that have well-known vulnerabilities. I don't know where they stand on their patches, or if they've even attempted to keep those up to date. As soon as we slap our company's name on that data, we become responsible for safeguarding it. Right now, I don't think we can do it. I'm not going to tell anyone in this room how to do their jobs, that's not my place, but what was decided on today assumes that everything is safe and

secure when that is absolutely not the case. I would ask that everyone assume nothing is safe and make their decisions based on that belief instead."

"If we made that assumption, we'd also be assuming your staff hasn't been doing their jobs," Russell said agitatedly, before he had the chance to stop himself. Even as the words left his tongue, he could feel Paul's demeanor next to him change. Oh well, he thought, sometimes honesty truly was the best policy.

Before Paul had a chance to say anything, Lisa was on her feet across the room. "That's an asinine claim and you know it! If everyone here wants to bury their heads in the sand and pretend that everything is peachy, that's fine, but don't try and say we aren't working our asses off on our end to try and fix this!"

"Lisa," Paul said quietly.

"No, Paul, this is crazy, and you know it! Literally everything that was decided today opens us up to more risks. If we go forward with any of these decisions, there will be hell to pay on the back end. The fact that anyone would consider making some of these changes blows my mind."

"Lisa!" Paul said, more forcefully this time.

Russell could feel his teeth grinding as he clenched his jaws together, listening to the accusations that were being thrown out. Finally, he had had enough. "Enough!" he said, slamming his open hand down on the desk. "Everyone, thank you for your hard work today. If you would please excuse me and Paul, that would be fantastic."

Silently, everyone stood and tried to make their way out the door as quickly as possible. Lisa remained by her seat, which only served to piss Russell off more than he already was. Finally, when the last of his staff had left and closed the door, Russell rounded on Paul, taking a moment of satisfaction in the shocked look on Paul's face.

"All I've heard from the both of you is problem after problem with little to no solutions. If you think there's a better way to do this, then speak up. If not, then let my staff do their jobs. It's not anyone in this room's place to decide if this deal goes forward. One way or another, it's happening, and you can either get on board or get the hell out! This meeting is over. Oh, and Paul," he said, taking a step closer to the CISO and lowering his voice to a menacing whisper, "I suggest you think long and hard next time before bringing one of your staff to openly insult me in one of my own meetings."

Russell could see the fury in Paul's eyes, but at least the man had the good sense not to act on it. Instead, he brushed past Russell without saying another word and walked out the door, Lisa following him after shooting one last hateful glare Russell's way.

Russell waited a few moments to make sure both were gone before sinking back down into his chair. There would most likely be hell to pay for what had just happened.

Chapter 4

Wednesday, 18 January

Brandon looked up from his computer when he heard the knocking on his door. Smiling, he waved Stacy in and closed his laptop, gesturing for her to take a seat.

"How are you doing today?" he asked, standing up and closing the blinds behind him so the sun wouldn't be shining directly in her face.

"I'm doing well. I've just been looking over some of these reports all morning."

"And?" he asked, walking across the room to pour them both a cup of coffee.

"The usual. Mitch is overestimating how much support his team will need. The various marketing team leads are all clamoring for new Business Intelligence analytics programs to better understand the new market we're entering. Russell's team is asking for intermediary systems to help with the merging of our and PGF's data. And I think Paul is going to have a heart attack before this is all over."

"Ah, yeah…" Brandon said, taking his seat and offering Stacy her cup, "I heard about his and Russell's exchange, if you want to call it that, last week. I've been meaning to pay the two of them a visit individually to try and see what's going on."

"I can save you the trouble," Stacy grimaced, rolling her eyes, "it's the same thing that always happens when those two are in the same room. Russell says everything is golden even when it's not, and Paul says the sky is falling even when it's not. Meanwhile, Mitch seems to think he can help diffuse the situation and has offered to help in whatever capacity you and I deem fit."

Brandon cocked his head inquisitively at that last comment. "What exactly does Mitch think he can do from his position?"

"I'm not sure," Stacy said with a sigh, "but based on the email he sent along with his budgetary requests he seems to think that a conflict between Russell and Paul is a significant concern and he wanted to have his concerns relayed through me to you. So, there it is. Mitch is concerned and wants to help."

Brandon chuckled and shook his head a bit. "Alright, Mitch's concern is noted. Aside from the three musketeers, you mentioned something about marketing wanting new analytics programs?"

"Yep. Marketing seems to think that this acquisition is going to require a lot more data analysis than they're prepared to execute. I personally think they are drastically underestimating their current capabilities, but I wanted to at least bring it up with you," Stacy said, absentmindedly rubbing her temples as she spoke.

Brandon nodded at that, "Why are people requesting new systems anyways? I thought it was made clear that we wouldn't be adding anything to the infrastructure during this process."

"I think everyone expects that they'll be given special treatment. In all reality, the comments we made last week had great intent, but the more I look at this, the more I realize we might need to make some exceptions. Our shareholders are going to expect immediate growth from this deal, which means we are going to have to be ready to move quickly as soon as we sign on the dotted line."

"Speaking of growth, you were there in the board meeting. Tom made it clear in no uncertain terms that he still expects us to beat Wall Street projections throughout this. What are your thoughts?" Brandon asked.

Stacy paused, her left index finger tapping thoughtfully on her upper lip while her right hand lazily circled the rim of her coffee cup. "I think we can do it. Or rather, I don't see any reason why we can't. It will just mean

being far more in control of our expenditures, tightening our belts, and keeping a handle on our projected ROI for projects we decide to undertake. Historically, some of our business managers have made decisions by the seat of their pants regarding projects. Sometimes they work and sometimes they don't, but there's more often than not very little analysis put in on the front end. We need to change that culture if we're going to do this without dropping the ball."

"How do you want to do it?"

"We need to force the issue. Before I approve any changes, they'll need to provide me and my staff with clear key performance indicators that they're trying to improve as well as a definitive projected ROI. No more wild claims. We'll need numbers from every leader. How much it's going to cost and how much revenue it's expected to generate. And, also, just between you and me, I think we need to focus on the quick earners for now as opposed to the long plays. A quick mid-range ROI will help us more than a long-term project with great ROI that won't pay out for years."

Brandon sighed a bit as he studied her, "Sometimes I wish you wouldn't speak so candidly like that. Could you imagine if we publicly stated that we were pursuing projects for short-term bumps in earnings as opposed to long-term stability?"

"Like I said... just between you and me. If you disagree, let me know and my staff can adjust accordingly."

"No, what you said makes sense. It's just unsettling to hear."

Stacy's slight smirk at that comment was the only indication she gave that she was pleased with his response. Reaching behind her, she grabbed a piece of paper that Brandon hadn't noticed her come in with.

"This is a list of the requested changes in budget. I didn't include the normal items since you and I had already agreed that those would remain constant. Rather, this is what's new since last week. I fully expect many

more items like this to come up as people have more time to think. The changes highlighted in red are the ones I recommend we reject. The ones in yellow are the ones for which I would need more of the details you and I just discussed. And the ones in green are the ones that line up with our current plans and I think we can go ahead and move forward on."

Brandon looked down over the paper she had handed him, taking in all the colors. "Damn," he finally muttered. "All of this was generated in the last few days? There's got to be at least two dozen items listed on this paper. I don't suppose anyone is asking for *less* money, are they?" He chuckled dryly at his joke, but he was already tallying up the numbers. Four items were highlighted in red, one item in green, and a whopping 21 other items were highlighted in yellow.

"Have you told any of the requestors that we would need more information?"

"I told them all that I wanted to discuss it with you before I gave out any additional information. Like I said, this will require a cultural shift in how we approach budgeting. I have no doubt that most people will refuse to put in the requisite work, which will move most of those yellows to red with minimal effort. The remaining few who do the work will be evaluated by my staff before I bring them back in here to you."

"You know some of the support functions are going to throw a fit about this new policy. Lisa already alluded to it in the last meeting about how they viewed ROI differently from what you and I are discussing."

"I wouldn't worry about Paul's team. They haven't requested any budgetary changes yet. I think between our meeting last week and his argument with Russell, Paul is trying to make all the changes he can in-house."

Brandon leaned back in his chair and stared up at the ceiling, wondering why he had been giving so much thought to his security team recently. Lisa's words had kept him thinking all weekend. This acquisition had to

go off without a hitch, and a security breach plastered across the news would certainly be an issue.

He commented, "Hell, with the Ransomware, third-party issues, and Nation State actions I keep reading about I'm surprised there's nothing yet."

"Let me know if Paul's team eventually comes back with any requests. If he can do it with what he's got, that's great, but if there's something important enough for him to stick his neck out again, I'll be interested in seeing what it is."

Stacy made a small note on her notepad before moving on to the rest of the meeting topics. Most of them were the usual updates to their financial standing as well as a comparison to some of their competitors in the marketplace. Brandon did his best to stay engaged, but he found himself making regular trips across the room to refill his coffee while Stacy continued to speak.

Outside his office, a TV hung in the waiting area on mute with the words scrolling lazily across the bottom of the screen. A news channel was reporting on a data breach at a manufacturing firm that had released all the personal and financial details of its thousands of employees. The company's name was being plastered across the screen with various "experts" weighing in on the damage.

Stacy continued talking in the background, saying something about stock price fluctuations overseas that may impact some of their customers. Brandon was hardly paying attention though, as the news continued displaying the breached company's name in big bold letters above the statement, "There were clear warnings that were ignored."

Shaking his head to snap himself out of his reverie, Brandon turned back to Stacy and nodded in what he hoped was a thoughtful manner, trying to show her that he was still paying attention. She looked at him a bit quizzically, but if she was put off by his actions, she didn't show it. Instead, she continued to speak about those damned stock fluctuations.

Finally, mercifully, after almost half an hour of speaking, she gave her overall assessment that WFG was fine, and assuming the market continued its current path, she estimated that they were in a supremely stable position. Brandon stood to escort her to the door and thanked her and her team for their hard work. Glancing outside he noticed that the news had moved on to a feel-good story about an animal shelter that had seen all its animals adopted by some private benefactor.

As Stacy walked out, Brandon said, "I agree with everything we discussed at the beginning of the meeting. I'll push out an email today underlining the cultural change that needs to take place as well as highlighting some of the things that need to be provided to your team. You have my full backing and if anyone gives you issues, send them my way. However, as I said, please let me know if Paul requests any changes. Consider it a morbid curiosity of mine."

Stacy nodded, thanked him for his support, and offered to send him key notes to include in his company-wide email before making her way to the elevator. He waited for the elevator doors to close before glancing at the TV one more time. Satisfied that it was showing happy pictures of the puppies being shown their new homes, he made his way back to his desk to start working on other issues.

Chapter 5

Paul locked eyes with Lisa, trying to ignore the open look of incredulousness on her face.

"Look, all I'm saying is that there is a certain level of tact that we need to use when discussing these issues with individuals outside our security department. I'm not saying I don't agree with your opinions, but twice now in the last week you've let your emotions get the better of you and have come close to openly berating executives in front of their staff. That needs to stop."

"Some of these people need to be berated! I'll do what you ask since I know you ultimately believe what I'm saying, but come on, Paul. The amount of attention these people place on security is less than the effort they put into deciding what type of coffee they want from Starbucks. It's embarrassing, and quite frankly, it's insulting as well."

Paul couldn't fault her there. Everything she was saying, and had been saying over the past week, was accurate. Her presentation skills just left a lot to be desired.

"Besides," she continued, "everyone is acting as though we are somehow secure in our current setup. I remember at least half a dozen times that either you or I have brought it to their attention that we are barely keeping our heads above the water. We're more proactive now than I think this company has ever been regarding security, but we still spend more than half our time doing triage. Changes aren't documented, infrastructure isn't updated, and there's no efficient way to track what is being done. We are staying afloat, but that's only because we've been sailing in calm waters. The moment we catch a wave, we're sunk for sure. Going public with this acquisition is asking to be hit. We might as well change our company logo to a giant target. The public is going to have

mixed reactions to this, and there will be those that love to hate us. We aren't prepared for them if they decide to react digitally."

"Okay, so what do you want to do about this aside from burning every bridge imaginable?" Paul cut in, acutely aware that if he let her keep going, she would be able to identify security shortcomings, most of them valid, for the rest of the day.

"Hundreds of things. If I had my way, we would be slamming on the brakes and fixing what's already broken before incurring more damage. But..." she paused, noting Paul's arched eyebrow, "since I know that's absolutely not going to happen, I suppose the next best thing would be to codify what we know is already broken on our end and attempt to better prepare for the new issues. Some of our problems may not be overly critical in the grand scheme of things, but others may prove to be much larger issues as soon as another organization is thrown into the mix."

Paul nodded thoughtfully. "A task force could be established to do that. You understand that you wouldn't get any additional funding for it though, right? You might be able to beg, borrow, cheat, and steal from some of the other project managers who may have some pennies lying around, but there's no way you'll be brought into the budget. Not with the current way things are going."

"Lucky for us, analysis is free," Lisa quipped, showing a sense of humor for the first time in a while. "We won't be implementing any solutions or making any changes. We'll just be trying to provide more ammunition for the next time you have to go toe to toe with Russell. One way or another, these people will come to understand security. I don't care if we have to spell it out to them letter by letter."

"I don't know if it will come to that, but we definitely need to do something to change the perception most people have about security here. I'm not going to lie, when I came over from the entertainment industry, part of the driving factor was that I expected people in finance to be far more security-aware. Instead, I find myself having to fight the

same fights that we fought more than five years ago at my old job. Even the analysis isn't free in this case. We are so short-staffed that every time you take people away from their primary jobs, we will be losing ground. Going forward, we will have to be extremely careful with our money management. Customer requests for security may take longer, your team is still on salary and being paid for a job we are taking them away from, and there is always the looming possibility of unplanned work. There's a book titled *The Phoenix Project* that I recommend you read. I picked it up this past weekend and it does a fantastic job of outlining the implications of unplanned work. You'll need to take all of that into account when constructing your agenda going forward. Between the M&A and existing projects already being funded, there may be some money left over somewhere. I may be able to convince Stacy to provide some cash for this down the road, but for now we'll have to make do with what we've already got.

Lisa jotted down a brief note on a piece of paper and pocketed it before replying. "I'll have the team come up with internal and external products. Hopefully, we can convince them that the lack of ROI is not equivalent to being useless. I would argue that preventing losses could be considered a return on investment if worded properly. As for the cost of doing this, I understand completely what you're getting at. I'll do my best to make sure nobody's time is wasted and that my team has a minimal impact on our ability to do our current projects. However, I'm sure you agree that this is something that most likely needs to be done sooner or later. I'd rather rip off the bandage now than keep kicking the can down the road."

"Agreed."

"Now," she said, leaning forward and lowering her voice a bit as though she was worried about being overhead, "I think there's another issue you and I should discuss in private before talking with others about it."

"And that is?" Paul asked, suddenly intrigued.

"Nobody has explicitly said it, but acquisitions of this size almost always lead to layoffs of some scale. There will be overlapping programs and the

board will decide that there's room to trim the fat. Running two organizations requires a lot more manpower than doubling the size of a single organization. There's going to be a lot of hurt feelings in both organizations when that happens. Prior to any official word being released about restructuring, I'd like to conduct a comprehensive review of account access privileges, monitoring capabilities, behavioral analytics, and anything else you can think of. The last thing we need is for an insider attack to blindside us while we're hardening ourselves against an external attack."

Paul laughed out loud at that, unable to control himself. "Either you're getting slow or I'm getting much better at this job than I give myself credit for. I've already discussed that issue with Maria, and her team is going to do the requisite checks. I need you and your new team to focus exclusively on the external issues as well as any infrastructure concerns. Maria will look internally and between the two of you, we should be able to not only defend what we've currently got but also develop a game plan for what's to come."

"Maria's team is good," she conceded, "but are you sure you wouldn't want both the internal and external looks being done by the same group? There may be some issues that impact both and it would be nice to have all of that centralized."

"I think you'll be busy enough as it is. Besides, this isn't just about looking towards the future. We still have a responsibility to do our current jobs, which means that this task force you'll be creating will be in addition to all your current responsibilities. Maria's team already handles access management for our internal staff, so it won't be too hard for her to also begin developing assessments. You're more than welcome to interface with her on key issues, but I want her staff leading that particular segment."

"Fair enough. I'll have a list of names for my task force before the end of today. Am I correct in assuming that they will also remain responsible for their old jobs as well as this new one?"

"You can poach two full-time resources, assuming they aren't critical to whichever team you are pulling them from. Preferably they come from two separate teams. For the rest, yes, you are correct. Remember, this is a project to help us get funding. If you do your job well enough, we might be able to fund a full-time team to handle this issue. How's that for incentive?"

"Good enough for me!" she said, grinning. "I'll keep you posted."

Paul watched her get up and leave his office before dropping his head and letting it hang there, the beginnings of a headache starting to creep in. Things certainly never seemed to get any easier. He hadn't been lying to her when he said he had expected things at WFG to be better than his old gig. How people in this day and age could treat security so carelessly confounded him. He was having to fight two struggles at once. Fix the security infrastructure that already existed while also having to convince everyone else to doing more than the bare minimum. And now, with this acquisition thrown into the mix, he honestly didn't see any way this would turn out alright. It wasn't a matter of if anything would happen, it was only a matter of how bad it would be. He only hoped that whatever powers that be, would be merciful.

A light knock on his door jolted him out of his thoughts. Maria stood there, smiling from ear to ear with a stack of papers in her hands.

"I've got an initial analysis on what we discussed," she said, waiting in the doorway.

"Ah, yes. Perfect, Maria. Please come in..." he said, gesturing to the same chair that Lisa had just vacated.

Chapter 6

Friday, 20 January

Stacy frowned slightly as she looked at some of the requests her staff was generating. There was more pushback from the key business units than she had anticipated when she rolled out the new requirements for budget requests. The initial friction had been expected, but people were still submitting the same requests time and time again without making any of the requisite edits. It was as though they were challenging her, seeing how long it would take before she caved and started handing out money. The email sent out by Brandon had done little to assuage any of the hostility and Stacy was growing concerned that the cultural shift she was hoping for was more of a dream and less of a reality.

She had no intent on backing down, however, and instead was drafting a memo to her staff that would essentially tell them to dig in their heels. The financial stability of this company for the foreseeable future depended on her staff's ability to ensure that any dollar being spent was generating more money on the back end. Her email pinged at her, reminding her of an upcoming meeting with Russell and Paul regarding their budget requests. Russell had been one of the biggest culprits so far, not even bothering to change the date on his requests as he forwarded them right back to her after they were sent back for revision. Paul hadn't submitted anything yet, although he had sent her a note asking how she defined ROI, as though that was a vague term open for interpretation. She wondered if this was the first time the two of them would be in the same room since their last episode. By now, news of that event had spread to the far corners of the building, and people were constantly on the lookout for the two of them interacting again.

Her computer pinged at her again, this time popping up a message from her receptionist letting her know that Paul had arrived. Rising from her chair to go greet him, she heard a second ping indicating that Russell too had arrived. Hopefully, if there was any hostility left between the two of

them, they wouldn't air it in her reception area. Opening her door, she welcomed both of them, ushering them inside quickly before closing the door again.

Russell was carrying a folder that was overflowing with documentation, which he threw on Stacy's desk before taking his seat. Paul, in contrast, was carrying no paperwork and instead smiled and waited for Stacy to return to her seat before taking his next to Russell.

"Gentlemen," she said, eyeballing the disorderly folder that had been deposited on her desk, "I trust everything is going alright for the both of you?"

"It's going great actually. How is everything going over here for you?" Russell asked, going through the motions but expressing no outward appearance that he actually cared how she was doing.

"Things are going well. With Brandon's blessing we've just rolled out a new system to track budgetary requests. It should help streamline certain processes as well as provide a more analytical approach to expenditures. Paul, how is everything going on your end?"

"As well as could be expected," Paul said, "Still trying to get my staff to wrap their minds around the implications of this acquisition."

"Makes sense. Speaking of which," Stacy said, feigning that she was studying an Excel document on her screen, "it appears as though we haven't gotten any budgetary requests pertaining to the acquisition from the security department. Is there a reason for that? I just want to make sure it isn't a fear of using our new system."

Out of the corner of her eye, she saw Russell roll his eyes before Paul had a chance to reply.

"Not at all," Paul said, either oblivious to Russell's faces or just choosing to ignore them. "I've got Maria looking at internal measures and Lisa looking at external measures. As far as tech solutions, we should have a proposed list for you shortly. They'll be prioritized by impact and

projected ROI. In our case, we are valuing the requests based off the money they save as opposed to the money they earn."

"And how are you measuring that?" Stacy asked, not thrilled by what she was hearing.

"Historical data. Sometimes we talk to the data owners personally to understand how they would value it. Additionally, we are looking at federal regulations and potential lawsuits as money-saving measures as well."

Russell openly scoffed at that, turning to Paul. "That's preposterous. With that math, each of your projects sounds like it will claim its ROI is equal to the value of this entire damn company."

Paul shrugged in response, apparently choosing to pay no attention to Russell's attitude. "Not quite that high, but yes, some of our higher priority items will have a substantial quantifiable and qualifiable ROI associated with them."

"Well, my requirements," Russell interjected, jabbing his finger in the direction of the folder on Stacy's desk, "all actually add value to this organization as opposed to just protecting us from some unseen masked intruder."

"Yes," Stacy said, happy for the opportunity to attempt to de-escalate what was occurring. "Let's talk about this folder. What is in it?"

"If you open it up, you'll see that it's a complete list of requirements my staff will need to pull off this acquisition. Most of it is to build redundancy in our networks in the event something fails during the consolidation, but other parts of it are required to allow our two networks to talk."

"And all of this is absolutely required?" Stacy asked, her frown deepening as she flipped through pages and pages of documented requirements, each seeming to be more expensive than the last.

"For the most part. If we're pinching pennies, there are some items I might be able to convince my staff we could do without, but there would be inherent risks in forgoing them."

"Of course. And are those risks documented? Has your staff listed out the return that we get for each of these investments?"

"Damn it, no. Do you see how many items there are in front of you? Going through item by item and attempting to generate some specific number would take a tremendous effort. My staff is already working to the bone as it is. All I can tell you is that the research has been put into each of these requests, and in every instance those items came back as either required or very highly recommended for us to be able to handle this acquisition without any hiccups."

"I understand it requires more work on the front end, but it should also make it easier on you in the long run. You'll be able to track project performance better by having a mark on the wall that was an agreed-upon goal. Besides, everyone else is going through the same pains you are. In the long run, my staff has to look at what's best for the business and not just at what's easiest to accomplish."

Russell looked like he had a smart comeback to that, but he must have decided it wasn't worth it because he simply grunted in acknowledgement and leaned back in his chair with his arms crossed.

"Now, as for security," Stacy said, pivoting her chair so that she was once again facing Paul. "From the sounds of it, you're at least trying to accomplish my goals of having a projected ROI tied to every investment. As... unique as some of your calculations may be, I appreciate the effort, nonetheless. Am I to assume that I'll have a list of budgetary requests from your staff before too long?"

"You are," Paul replied. "However, in the interim, one of the reasons we are slower than some of the other units in getting you our requests is a manning issue. The task force I've put together to tackle this issue is being pulled from other sections in my staff, and the people running it are still

responsible for their other jobs. If I could get approval for three more full-time employees, I could get all this work through to you much faster. As it stands, we are struggling just to meet our current requirements without projecting forward like you're asking. It can be done, but it won't be pretty. My initial request from you would be for funding for additional help – say $300,000 just to be safe. I can get you the projected ROI for their output if you'd like."

"For the sake of appearances, please go through the motions of projecting out what additional help would do for your section. Your argument sounds compelling, but I'll have to put this in front of HR and Brandon before I can officially sign off on it."

Paul nodded, apparently satisfied with her answer.

Looking back and forth between the two of them sitting in front of her, Stacy could practically feel the tension between them. Paul tried to act nonchalant, and Russell was doing everything in his power not to look to his left, but it was evident. Stacy made a mental note to follow up with Brandon on her observations as well as to inform him of Paul's current stance on security. The two of them, apparently concluding that the meeting was over at the same time, stood up in unison. If the situation had been tense before, now it was just awkward as they attempted to slide by each other and make a line towards the door. Stacy couldn't help but shake her head as she watched the two grown men act like this. Still, what little humor she felt was quickly dashed as her computer pinged at her, opening an email from Mitch complaining about why his requests were being sent back to him.

Chapter 7

Thursday, 16 March

Paul stared at the flashing red icons on his screen, subconsciously running his fingers through his hair as he willed them to turn green. How the hell was this still happening? He knew this thing was bad when it had originally started that morning, but he hadn't expected it to be this bad. The hits kept coming, and his team was scrambling to do damage control while also trying to solve the issue at hand. The defacement of the website was first, but now there seemed to be a parallel Distributed Denial of Service (DDoS) attack impacting the customer-facing services as well. He thought to himself, "What's next, ransomware on top of this?"

Lisa's team had relocated over to Russell's wing of the building to aid in rerouting the traffic and blocking all the malicious traffic. The rest of his staff was trying to lock everything down, preventing any more unwanted changes to the website. When the website had come back online the first time, everything had been altered and replaced with a political message. Paul hadn't had the chance to read it in-depth, but from what he had seen, clearly someone was not happy about this acquisition.

His phone suddenly started buzzing on his desk, almost vibrating itself off the edge. In large white letters, the name "BRANDON" was displayed across the screen. Paul cringed and reached towards the phone. This was the fourth time Brandon had called him since this attack had begun less than two hours ago.

"This is Paul," he said, pushing the speakerphone button and setting the phone back on his desk.

"Paul, it's Brandon. Just wanted to see if your staff had an update."

Paul pinched the bridge of his nose and squeezed his eyes shut, willing himself to breathe evenly so that his frustration wasn't evident on the phone.

"Not since the last time we spoke, Brandon. Russell's crew is working on getting everything re-routed and getting us back online. I've got Lisa and her staff over there making sure nothing is sneaking in through the cracks while we all focus on this attack. We've got drills in place for DDoS hits, it's just a matter of going through the appropriate steps."

"Do we know who is doing this yet?"

"Brandon, to be honest, I don't know who it is, nor do I care right now. Russell's crew is working to get us functioning again and my crew is focused on making sure they aren't going to blindside us with something else. The 'who' and 'why' will have to come later. The DDoS attack was relatively easy to deflect with our outsource services once it was identified. As for the website defacement, we are working to identify how it happened. We may never be able to accurately identify the source of all this. For now, my team's focus is on shutting this thing down."

"Paul, listen damn it, I want to know who's responsible for this. And I want to know why they're able to do this much damage to us."

Paul stared at his phone incredulously for a few moments, clenching and unclenching his fists as he tried to collect his thoughts for a response. "Brandon, I understand your frustration. How they were able to alter the website is a big unknown right now, and as soon as we have time to breathe, we will dig into that. As for the denial of service we're experiencing, there's no easy way to limit this amount of traffic. The best we can do is respond to it. We should be back up and running shortly. That's more in Russell's lane. Like I said, my biggest concern is that whoever this is doesn't extract some data or leave something behind."

Paul could actually hear Brandon sigh through his speakerphone. Finally, he said, "Fine. That makes sense. I'll leave this to you and Russell to handle. When this is over with, both of you come see me so I can get to the bottom of this. The board is going to want to know everything. Our customers are going to want to know more. What they wrote on our website is patently false, and I will not stand to have such overt slander spread for everyone to read."

The call went dead, leaving Paul staring at the phone in confusion. When things slowed down, he would definitely have to go back and dissect what was put on their webpage. In the interim, he really hoped that was the last time Brandon called him during this ordeal. It wasn't the fact that the CEO was calling him every twenty minutes so much as it was the fact that Brandon clearly didn't understand the delineation of responsibilities between Paul and Russell.

Paul had had to bite his tongue during one of his earlier phone calls with Brandon after it was insinuated that had Paul's staff done a better job, they could have been more prepared for this. Maybe if his damn budget request had been approved, Paul would have had the staff to do everything. He still couldn't believe that his request for more manning for Lisa's task force had been disapproved. That had been a little over two months ago, but it still bothered him every day as he walked into an ever-growing list of things that he was forced to ignore due to manning constraints.

There had been a generally positive response to WFG's public announcement back in January, but Lisa's task force and their Threat Intel partners had already identified key points of concern that indicated there may be a retaliatory attack by some hacktivists. Something about some less than stellar customer service in WFG's past had come back into the public as Wall Street analysts had dug into both WFG and PGF. Brandon had brought that concern up at a meeting with the rest of the executive staff and had received positive feedback from Russell. Both of their staff had dug into the concern and continued to monitor it, but this was the first time that their prediction had come to fruition.

The DDoS had started immediately after lunch, impacting their external-facing services and sending Brandon and the IT crew into a controlled panic. Paul and his staff had begun helping with traffic control at that point, as well as scanning to see if any other activities were going on in other parts of the network. When the website went down, everyone had assumed it was someone else in the organization trying to mitigate the damage. Miscommunication between the business units involved hadn't

helped, and when the website finally came back up defaced, Brandon had gotten involved. Paul was sure Russell was also getting hammered by Brandon and probably feeling just as frustrated as Paul at being distracted from emergency management by having to explain every step he took.

Paul looked up to see both Maria and Lisa poking their heads into his office.

"Want an update?" Lisa asked cheerfully. Evidently, she was enjoying the situation, no doubt viewing it as some form of vindication.

"Absolutely. Both of you come on in."

Lisa started speaking first as she took her seat. "Russell's team more or less has it figured out. There were a few moments where it looked like they had their heads up their asses, but I have to admit, Russell and some of his crew managed to keep the ship steady and keep everyone on the right track. As much as I hate to say it, it was impressive. We should be good in the next thirty or so minutes, assuming something catastrophic doesn't happen."

Maria chimed in as soon as Lisa had finished speaking, "We didn't see anything entering or leaving the network. My staff is going to continue to scan, but I feel safe in saying that their main goal was to knock us off our feet, not to steal any information. I don't know if you read what they put on our webpage, but whoever this is clearly isn't a fan. This was probably more of a socio-political statement than anything else."

"I've read it. Not flattering, and definitely someone with a longstanding grudge," Paul said. "I'm interested to see if this is in line with what we thought was a key risk. At the very least, it will prove that we were thinking on the right track. After this has settled down, both of you please send me a report of your respective functions during this. Brandon is going to want a roll-up and I think it would be good to formalize some of the processes we went through. Also, please identify key measures that would have offered additional protection against this. Budget requests

are always easier to get pushed through after an event like this, as long as we leverage what we know to show that there are key items that will help prevent it from happening again. I don't want to overwhelm them with requests and have them feel that we're taking advantage of the situation, so for now please make sure that all proposed requests tie directly back to today's events."

The conversation after that turned to key lessons learned for both of their respective staffs. All in all, Paul was pleased with how the security staff had operated. While everyone else had panicked, it seemed that both Lisa's and Maria's teams had remained mostly level-headed. The key would be to capture these points while they were fresh in everybody's mind and document them in a way to be readily understood by the rest of the executive leadership as well as update all the Run Books. Incident response was something everyone had said they were prepared for, but the day's events had proven that some had put more of an effort into it than others. Both Maria and Lisa made relevant points and promised to have their staff provide details all the way down to the lowest level.

Halfway through their discussion, Paul received an email requesting his attendance at a post event review with Brandon at 9:00 a.m. the following morning. Glancing at his watch, he realized that it was going to be another late night. There seemed to be more and more of those lately.

Chapter 8

Friday, 17 March

"Changes were made without any form of authorization or checks and balances. We can only protect what we know about, and yesterday my staff was discovering new applications, systems, and devices to secure while still trying to contain the issue at hand. Having to make decisions like that on the fly is incredibly risky and could have easily been prevented if we had just instituted a system of checks and balances as well as a coherent change management strategy. Clearly, we were ill-prepared to handle the incident. I recommend we bring in some external consultants to walk us through the best systems and processes to run if we ever experience something like yesterday again. All of that should have been done prior to now, but I think it's better late than never. My team is already drafting up the budget requirements for all those recommendations."

Russell could feel his blood pressure rising as he listened to Paul throwing him under the bus. How dare he sit there with a straight face and tell Brandon that the blame rests with anyone other than himself. They had gotten breached! There was no one else who deserved to be thrown under the bus more than the security staff that had failed to do their damn jobs.

"Russell, do you have any thoughts on that proposal?" Brandon asked, turning towards both him and Charlotte.

"You're damn right I do. First of all, I refuse to sit here and have it insinuated that this was in any way, shape, or form my issue. Our systems got hit and my staff immediately responded to the emergency in the most effective and efficient way, shutting down the attack and mitigating any future issues. If we were vulnerable, that's a security shortcoming, not mine. Secondly, we have a change management system that tracks all changes. Just because other organizations don't come actively looking for

it doesn't mean it doesn't exist. I can't be expected to do my job while simultaneously having to spoon-feed everyone else."

"Your change management process, if you want to call it that, does us no good," Lisa interjected, leaning forward behind Paul. "All it does is track changes that have already been made. There's no preapproval process that looks at the security implications. We got hit yesterday because we have gaps and holes. Those don't just randomly appear. They're a result of making decisions about IT architecture by the seat of your pants!"

Charlotte let out a sharp laugh to Russell's left. "You honestly expect anyone in here to believe that we don't have an approval process? Who are you trying to kid? Just because your staff hasn't ever felt the need to help doesn't mean we haven't taken it upon ourselves to pick up the slack. My team looks at all changes from multiple perspectives, to include security."

"Clearly, they aren't doing a good job of it," Lisa retorted.

Russell saw Paul wince at Lisa's comment, obviously recognizing the trap she had walked into.

"They're doing a better job of it than your staff is doing, which is to say, they're actually trying to do the job!" Charlotte shot back.

Lisa reeled back as though she had been physically struck, her mouth opening and closing without words coming out. Russell might have found it a comical sight had it not been occurring in what should have been a serious meeting.

"Easy, you two," Brandon said, holding up his hands and trying to deescalate the situation. "The intent of this isn't to attack each other. I just want to come up with both a summary of what happened as well as a list of viable actions that will prevent it from happening again."

"I think you're getting that," Paul replied, speaking evenly. "Clearly, there is a lack of communication between Russell's staff and mine. They're making changes and driving ahead with projects, and we aren't informed

enough to do our jobs. We can sit here and point fingers all we want, and I'll admit that's partly my fault, but if we want to come up with something productive out of this meeting, then I suggest we focus on that key issue. How do we flatten the communication channels between IT and security so that the two work in tandem as opposed to the clearly conflicting working relationship they currently have?"

Russell's eyes narrowed as he studied Paul. What game was he playing? There was no way he really meant that touchy-feely communication bullshit.

"How exactly do you propose we do that?" he asked, noticing that Brandon was watching this exchange intently.

"I don't have a complete framework built out in my mind. That's something both you and I need to work on and come to a consensus on. All I know is we need to formalize processes between the two of us. Whatever we decide on, it needs to go beyond change management. It needs to encompass that plus continual security audits and incident response procedures. We are two separate and distinct staffs, but we interact enough for there to be a systematic approach to how we do business."

"I think a sync meeting would be a good place to start," Charlotte said, slightly scooting forward in her chair so that she could speak to Paul around Russell.

Paul nodded slightly. "I think so too. I think the focus of the first few meetings needs to be on establishing a baseline of roles and responsibilities. As you so ... aptly identified, your staff has taken it upon themselves to fill in for my staff's perceived shortcomings."

Charlotte fidgeted awkwardly in her seat at being reminded of her harsh comments mere moments before. She seemed to be going out of her way to avoid eye contact with Lisa and was at a loss for words.

To save her further discomfort, Russell turned back towards Paul and Lisa and asked, "What makes you think my staff isn't capable of handling it ourselves?"

"For starters – yesterday's events," Paul said, locking eyes with Russell. "I don't mean any offense by that; it was just as much a security failure as it was an IT failure. But clearly what we're doing now isn't working, and with the pending acquisition, your staff is only going to get busier. Let my crew do their job. The only thing I ask is that what we come back with in the way of recommendations and requirements is taken seriously. It seems like everything we've said to date has gone in one ear and come right back out the other, and we paid the price for that yesterday. The only way we're going to get after this problem is through collaboration."

"We developed some ad hoc procedures yesterday," Lisa said. "My staff worked with Will and his staff in IT and were able to work together easily. There were some minor issues, but nothing we weren't able to immediately get past. I would say that if we were able to do that on a larger scale, we would be moving in the right direction."

She continued, "Will and his staff did a good job of looking at the IT tech issues while my staff helped work on the security issues. There was very little friction and between the two groups we were able to get out ahead of the problem. I doubt his staff or my staff could have done that alone in an entire day, let alone in the few hours we had."

"We do a director huddle on Monday mornings at 9. Do you guys do something similar on your end?" Charlotte asked.

"We do. Ours starts at 8:30 and normally lasts until right around 9:30," Lisa replied.

"What if we did a cross org sync meeting at 10:30 then? That gives our guys enough time to issue guidance to their staff after our meeting. We can sync on Monday mornings and discuss ongoing and future projects. It may not be a final solution, but it's a start."

"I'll attend the first few, just to see how it works for myself," Russell said. "However, Paul, I recommend you and I do an individual sync separately at some point during the week as well. Some of the problems are more than just communication issues, and I think you and I need to take a good, honest look at what those are."

Paul nodded in agreement, pulling out his phone and opening the calendar. "How does Tuesday morning work for you? It'll give them time to have their meeting on Monday and present any pertinent issues to us. We should be able to take action by Tuesday."

"Agreed," Russell said. "I'll send you a calendar notice after this."

Brandon clapped his hands excitedly from the front of the room, earning a surprised jump from Lisa, Paul, Russell, and Charlotte. Russell had forgotten the CEO was even in the room, and it seemed as though the rest of the group had as well.

"I'm thrilled to be seeing this teamwork!" Brandon beamed. "If you guys can accomplish half as much as you are planning, I think it's going to be awesome. I challenge both of your staffs to not constrain themselves to solving current problems, but to also work to identify and prevent future problems. If you can do that, which I have no doubt you can, then I think this acquisition is going to go off without a hitch. Now, I hate to cut things short, but Stacy is due here any minute and I'm sure she's going to be a joy to listen to. You're more than welcome to stay for her financial update, but I would recommend you escape while you still can."

He gave them each a wink, as though he were letting them in on a shared secret with his comments, almost causing Russell to involuntarily groan. He caught himself at the last minute, though, and instead replied with a chuckle. At least Brandon wasn't berating his staff like he had yesterday. That had been a nightmare to endure while trying to solve the issue.

"I think I'm going to have to pass on that particular party," Russell said. "So, if you'll excuse me and Charlotte, we're going to get out of here. Paul

and Lisa, it was a pleasure to speak with you this morning. We will see both of you on Monday for the kickoff of the sync meeting."

"Let's say each of these columns represents a week. That means by the end of these four sections we will be exactly one month from today. I vote we start drafting up a plan of reasonable goals that we can hit over the next four weeks and start working on those issues. I think the most logical place to start is a review of patches to make sure they were all implemented. Conservatively, that will probably take two weeks between our two staff." She drew a horizontal line through the first two columns and wrote *Patch Review* above it.

"Concurrently with that, I think we can start coming up with a communication system that streamlines the entire process. I don't have an idea right now off the top of my head, but I can't imagine it will be too hard to come up with. I think it should only take a week to get an idea and then the remainder of the month to implement and educate people on the new system." She drew two more horizontal lines on the white board. The first one was in the first column and had *Communication Development* written above it. The second horizontal line started in the second column and stretched to the far edge of the whiteboard with *Communication Process Implementation* written above it.

"And finally," Lisa continued, "I think after our patch review, we should identify any holes that were left by faulty patch management and work to fix those." She drew a fourth horizontal line across the last two columns and wrote *Patching/Updating & Configuration Management* above it.

Will nodded energetically next to her and said, "I think that's about as much as we can handle in one month's time, but if we are able to accomplish all of that, then we will be in a much better place in four weeks than we are right now."

"I agree," Charlotte said. "I don't want to try and do too much at once, but I think what you've outlined is definitely manageable. I think everyone in this room agrees that there are dozens if not hundreds of issues that will ultimately need to be addressed and fixed. However, I

think you've identified some of the critical shortcomings and those should absolutely be the priority."

Maria raised her hand. "My only concern is whether or not you're being overly optimistic with your time assessments. We don't know for sure how successful or unsuccessful we have been at implementing all patches we planned for. Two weeks may be more than enough time to do the review, but it could just as easily be too short."

"I want you all to be aggressive for now in your approach to timelines," Paul said from his seat along the wall. "Purely from a business perspective, the faster we handle these issues, the better off we are. However, also view it as a test and validation of this new work agreement between the two orgs. While this may seem aggressive to some, I'd rather work the issues out now during a project that we control than during a real-world incident response."

Lisa noted the wide-eyed response that many of the IT managers and security managers gave Paul. Clearly, they hadn't been expecting this to turn into a stress test. Still, what Paul was saying made sense and Lisa saw most of the individuals in the room begrudgingly nodding their heads in agreement. This was a new form of collaboration, and it would pay dividends if they were able to formalize their processes prior to having to react to an emergency. Besides, having Paul's support for her proposed timeline was going to make it much easier to enforce amongst her peers.

Lisa was almost too busy watching the reactions amongst the IT managers to notice the wink that Paul passed Maria. Maria nodded and smiled back, putting her phone back in her pocket. Lisa hadn't seen her take her phone out. Had she had it out before she asked her question? Could her question have been purposefully phrased to set Paul up for his comment? Lisa wouldn't put it past Paul to have worked to orchestrate that moment. This was the perfect place to exert some of his influence over the IT staff without having to worry about a dissenting opinion from Russell. Lisa couldn't help but wonder at just how crafty Paul was.

She stared at Paul and waited for him to make eye contact before glancing at Maria and back at him inquisitively. He just grinned sheepishly and gave a halfhearted shrug before going back to whatever he was doing on his phone. Lisa looked around the room once more. It appeared that nobody else had observed the nonverbal exchanges that had just taken place, so she contented herself with listening in as some of the other IT and security managers began excitedly discussing specific plans to meet her requirements listed on the board. She made a mental note to talk to both Paul and Maria later about what specifically had just transpired.

Chapter 11

Tuesday, 21 March

Paul knocked lightly on the doorframe and stepped into the office, making sure he was smiling as Brandon looked up from his keyboard.

"Paul!" Brandon exclaimed. "Come in! Come in! Please make yourself comfortable. Can I interest you in a cup of coffee?" he asked, gesturing towards the coffee machine atop the counter on the other side of the room.

"Uh, no thanks. I'm good," Paul said, sitting down in front of Brandon and wondering not for the first time why he had been cryptically summoned to Brandon's office early in the morning to discuss "security considerations".

"So, I bet you're wondering why I called you here," Brandon said with a smile as though he could read Paul's mind. "Fact is, I don't really have an agenda, just a purpose. I had a discussion recently about WFG. The general theme of the conversation was the fact that as a company, we are doing wonderfully."

"Well, that's great to hear..." Paul said, wondering if this diatribe was some sort of punishment for him turning down the coffee.

"Fact is, we're doing wonderfully in every single of our business units except security. In that regard, it would appear as though we are struggling."

Paul froze and stared at Brandon.

"Relax," Brandon said, looking at Paul with a concerned expression. "This isn't a negative review about your performance. If you and I are both being honest, you have gone above and beyond in trying to educate everyone about security concerns. We, or more specifically I, just haven't been listening as well as I should have."

Brandon took a sip of his coffee and actually briefly looked nervous before continuing. "I guess what I'm trying to say is you have my attention now. If there's anything you want to say that you think I need to be aware of, now's the time to mention it. You have my undivided attention."

"To be completely honest, I wish I would have known this was the topic of conversation today. I could have come with an entire list of things to talk about," Paul said.

"That's exactly why I didn't tell you what we would be talking about," Brandon replied, "I didn't want you coming here with an extensive list and have you walk me through each point line by line. I want to have a discussion. It may be a little unorthodox, but humor me. Let's talk about what your concerns are."

"Well, to be quite frank, and speaking off the cuff, I'd say my biggest concern is the integration of security into the business as a whole. As you said, we are very good at getting the job done when it comes to capturing market share and expanding our product offering, but we do some of those things at the expense of security. I'm not saying we need to cut product offerings, I'm just saying that as we continue to increase in scope and size, our security infrastructure needs to expand accordingly."

Brandon nodded thoughtfully but remained silent, prompting Paul to keep speaking.

"I think we'll get the biggest bang for our buck by better syncing up security and IT. Our IT systems support almost everything we do, and if we secure those critical assets, then it will be much easier for us to identify threat vectors and respond accordingly. A big reason the recent attack was able to take place was a failure of IT and security to remain in line with each other. We fell out of alignment and allowed critical job functions to fall by the wayside, which left us vulnerable to a threat that we should have been protected against."

"Speaking of your staff and Russell's, how did yesterday morning's meeting go?" Brandon asked.

"It went well. From my perspective, the directors and managers did a great job at identifying critical gaps and started working on solutions. They outlined a month-long project timeline that should hopefully have us on much better footing regarding security. Additionally, each of those tasks was broken down into more granular tasks that should take at most five days. That way they are always working towards a short-term problem and can see results much more rapidly."

"And Russell? What did he think of it?"

Paul paused, his mind racing to formulate a response to the seemingly innocuous question.

"He, uh, couldn't make it. It's understandable, honestly; everyone is swamped with the upcoming acquisition. I have no doubt that he's slammed with work. As far as I'm aware, our meeting for this afternoon is still on. I should be able to get a better gauge as to his feelings on the matter then."

"I see," said Brandon, frowning slightly as he ran his finger along the rim of his coffee cup.

Paul sat there silently waiting for more, but it never came, leaving the both of them staring at each other awkwardly. After a few moments of hesitation, Paul pressed on wanting to leave the unspoken feelings about Russell alone.

"In all reality, I don't think the security situation here is as dismal as you may think," Paul said, taking note of the somewhat surprised and amused look on Brandon's face. "We may be far behind when it comes to patch management and the implementation of security measures along our perimeter, but our incident response process is fairly mature, all things considered. When our Vulnerability and Asset Management teams identify a problem, we are quick to pounce on it and get rid of it. The next logical step is to set up defense mechanisms that help prevent attacks from ever occurring, but in all reality, if we had to choose between being

weak in incident response or weak in security software, I'd choose our current setup any day of the week."

"That makes sense," Brandon said. "I know you and your staff are working tirelessly to keep us safe and that it may not always seem as though your work is appreciated. Part of the reason I wanted to have this discussion today is to hopefully fix that misconception. The executive leadership here, me specifically, understands the need for security. The issue so far has been a matter of having full faith and confidence that we aren't spending money just to spend money. You've done a good job so far of highlighting some key concerns, but at the end of the day, the business leadership needs a way to validate spending money to fix those concerns. To be completely candid, I hear conflicting advice from you, Russell, the news, and my peers daily. Obviously, I defer to you in most cases since it's your job, but it's not always clear where the mixed signals are originating from. With that in mind, assuming you had the resources allocated to you, what would your next steps be to help provide some clarity?" he asked.

Paul thought about it for a few moments, collecting his thoughts before responding.

"I'd need the manpower to spin out a strategic planning team. That's where I would start. Right now, all my resources are devoted to keeping us running. I don't have the ability to get my head far enough above water to begin planning and forecasting out nearly as far as I should be. I'm doing you and the company a disservice by being as reactive as I am. If I had a few more people who were able to identify potential future issues, then I could begin implementing solutions today and get out ahead of the issues. At that point I think you, me, Stacy, and Russell would have to sit down and talk about a few key decision points."

"Such as?"

"First of all," Paul replied, "after we give ourselves some room to maneuver, I'd like to take a hard look at what we are responsible for internally and try to do away with projects that sap our manpower but

don't provide a comparable benefit. A cost-benefit analysis on all our security systems and projects, so to speak. Ultimately, I'd like to be able to provide you with a list of items we absolutely must keep in-house, items we could easily get away with pushing off to external parties, and items that have some risks and rewards for doing either."

"So, you want to increase manpower only to be able to determine what projects you can cut?" Brandon asked, smiling.

Paul let out a short laugh and said, "Let me try to clarify that. I want the manpower to allow us to strategically plan and guide us into the future. I want to shed unnecessary work so that we can focus on the really important stuff. The other items are important, but they can be done by someone else and help free up some of my overworked staff. Once we've gotten to that point, we can start implementing the solutions that my strategy staff is identifying. Some of the solutions will be created in-house and others will be outsourced, but sooner or later we will be much more focused and streamlined, able to secure all assets on our network. We aren't there yet, but it's absolutely possible. My team just needs the support structures in place to allow us to do our job."

"And you don't feel like the support you've gotten has been adequate?" Brandon asked.

For a brief moment, Paul considered giving a noncommittal answer. Instead, he decided that honesty was the best policy considering how the conversation had been going. "To be honest, no. We haven't been given the funding we've requested and that's caused us to have issues. I can't guarantee it, but we probably could have prevented the last attack had some of my funding requests been approved. I think if I can get the resources I need and the working relationship with Russell that I'm hoping for, then I'll be able to provide a much more efficient and effective security solution."

"Alright," Brandon said, holding up his hands, "that was a very candid and well-received answer. You understand that Stacy will want hard numbers to support your claims, correct?"

"That's one of the primary concerns of mine," Paul replied. "We've been providing some hard numbers, but security isn't an exact science. We don't always see what we prevent from occurring, and we can't predict the number or impact of them until they happen."

"True, if you look at it myopically. But what about the business? What are you really protecting and how do you know what next year's threats will be? I understand that you want us to buy things that are required by regulation, and I completely support that. But for everything else, you need to convince us that there is a real and tangible threat as opposed to simply trying to spend money to defend against every possible eventuality."

Paul nodded. "I understand what you're saying, and I completely agree. I just don't know if that data can be formatted the way you expect."

"CIOs have been doing this for years," Brandon said. "They tie it to the business and the technology requests. Even though they have a slightly easier time of it since they support or drive revenue more than you do, it should be a similar process"

Paul realized this wasn't the time to start a disagreement, so he acquiesced. "Makes sense. I'll get with Russell after this and see if I can pull out some of his methods for getting the numbers and apply them to my needs."

"Good, well then, if you can provide Stacy with those numbers, then you have my full support to make the changes you mentioned. I'll talk with her to make sure she understands my intent on this. I want you to be given the opportunity to deliver on the promises you made. If you get pushback from any of the other business owners, to include Russell, try and handle it at your level. If it proves to be too big a hurdle to manage, bring it to my attention and I'll kill the issue. If we can become as secure as you alluded to prior to this acquisition taking place, then I'll sleep a lot more comfortably at night."

"I'll work on getting those numbers to Stacy after my meeting with Russell this afternoon. I'm confident that he and I will be able to see eye to eye on a good number of the issues and create a plan that will help fix both of our issues at once," Paul said.

"That sounds great!" Brandon exclaimed, seeming overly upbeat. "I appreciate you finding the time to come talk about this. I know it was last minute. I look forward to seeing what you and your crew can accomplish and look forward to receiving updates."

Taking the cue that the meeting had come to a close, Paul thanked Brandon for the vote of confidence and made his way out of the CEO's office, thinking about the list of topics he wanted to discuss with Russell this afternoon. He had put on a positive face in front of Brandon, but he still harbored doubts about the working relationship between himself and the CIO. The meeting this afternoon could go one of two ways, and after Russell's no-show yesterday morning he had a sinking feeling he knew which way the meeting would go.

Chapter 12

Tuesday, 21 March

"Wait, wait, wait. You're telling me you got funding approved just like that? All because you told Brandon some sob story about being understaffed?! And now you want me to give you my metrics so that you can repackage them and take more money from me?" Russell asked incredulously. "Are you kidding me? I've been telling him and Stacy that I need more resources for months now and all I ever get is a budget request kicked back in my face, asking for more details."

"It hasn't been officially approved. He just told me that I had his support in making necessary changes. And for the record, it wasn't a sob story, it was just a laydown of what my staff needed to meet his expectations."

Russell couldn't believe what he was hearing. For starters, why was Paul having discussions relating to IT with the CEO without him? And now, to top it off, he was finding out that somehow Paul had been given carte blanche with the budget while he himself was continually having to argue his case with Stacy.

"Yeah, I get that," Russell shot back. "But his expectations are based on a false sense of what the underlying issues are. We have ample security measures in place. We employ firewalls, we have network intrusion devices, and we utilize the best access control methods possible, as per your staff's recommendations, I might add. Our issue isn't the fact that we don't have enough security systems; it's the fact that my staff is having to make do with outdated and broken systems that can't keep up with business demands. And yet, every time I bring that up to Brandon or Stacy, I get told that I need to provide more details. This is bullshit and you know it."

Paul let out a long sigh before replying. "Look, Russell, I can see why you're upset about this, but the fact is that half the systems you're referencing are outdated themselves. Security measures that we don't

continually update eventually turn into liabilities rather than assets. This is a perfect example of why I think we need to work more closely together as opposed to how we've worked in the past."

"And yet you went and talked to Brandon without me," Russell snapped.

"Yes, Brandon invited me to his office for a meeting. Had I known what it was about, I would have asked you to attend as well. Trust me when I say I was just as blindsided by the topic as you are now. But moving past that, I'd like to discuss a few key concerns of mine. You highlighted a lot of the security features we employ currently and alluded to the fact that they were good enough. I would argue that they aren't. I told Brandon the nontechnical side of the story, but speaking security to IT right now, I think how we manage our security infrastructure leaves a lot of holes. We are spending a lot of money protecting our network when that's not even the real target. Anyone who attempts a breach will use the network as a vector but will ultimately be targeting our data, which we do next to nothing to protect right now. We need to safeguard data both at rest and in transit, and we need to implement a proper data classification and sensitivity program throughout the company. We also need to take a good, hard look at our identity and access management processes to ensure people only have the access and entitlements they require to do their job. Some teams seem to have taken too much liberty with the access levels they've been handing out to their staff. We aren't doing that now, but we need to be."

Russell clenched and unclenched his fists a few times under the table. "That makes a great sales pitch, and I have no doubt that's why you're suddenly getting this funding, but you're forgetting that last week's attack was a DDoS. The target was the network."

"And the website," Paul added quietly.

"Yes! And the damn website! But what I'm getting at here is that we can't just keep pouring money into hunting some made-up threat when the infrastructure may not be able to continue operating. God knows who is setting the priorities in this place, but I don't know what they expect you

to secure if I can't develop the IT architecture. Keep our firewalls up and running and let me develop the infrastructure that needs to be built. It's that simple."

For a second, Russell thought Paul was about to back down and agree. Instead, he grabbed a piece of paper off his desk and turned it so that it faced Russell. "Let's assume this is the firewall," Paul said, drawing a circle on the paper in pencil. "Every time we need to let an application interact with your systems, every time we do business and partner interactions, and every time we allow remote access, we have to poke holes in it." Paul punctuated his comments by erasing segments of the circle. "What we are left with is an extremely porous security system that deters the casual attacker but does nothing against our more motivated adversaries." Paul slid the paper across the desk towards Russell, who looked down and saw a series of dashed lines surrounded by smudge marks from the eraser. The shape on the paper was barely recognizable as a circle anymore.

Paul continued, "What about insiders? Collaboration and collusion? There are multiple things we need to be looking for and protecting ourselves against."

Russell placed his hand on the paper and slid it firmly back towards Paul, leaning forward across the desk. "Let me let you in on a little secret, Paul, because it appears you have forgotten yourself. My job is IT and I'm damn good at it. I know how a damn firewall works. The next time you want to teach me a lesson as though I'm a child, I suggest you think long and hard about the point you're trying to make. I came here today to try and mend the rift that was forming between us. Instead, you go behind my back to Brandon and steal all my money. If you want to pretend like the sky is falling, be my guest, but I'm going to continue operating in the real world and work to make sure this acquisition happens according to plan. I'll let you explain to Brandon why we failed if you continue to get in my way."

"Russell, I think you're misunderstanding me here. I'm not trying to get in your way; I'm trying to collaborate on this. I wasn't trying to be demeaning, I was trying to let you know what my concerns are in our

current security posture. I'm trying to enable you to do your job, not hinder you. All I need is for us to be speaking the same language when we present it to Brandon and Stacy," Paul said, holding his hands up.

"You have my support for our managers and directors to continue their meetings. And if there's ever an emergency, we can try this again. But for now, I've got more important things to do than sit here and entertain every security concern," Russell replied, standing up and making his way to the door.

He half expected to hear a word of protest from Paul, but instead there was just silence as he exited Paul's office. He was furious, but the more he thought about it, the more he wasn't sure who he was furious at. Paul hadn't said anything that wasn't true, but the fact that he had gone behind Russell's back to secure funding had been a slap in the face.

He arrived back in his office far calmer than he had been when he left Paul's. During his walk he had made a few key decisions about how he would go forward. First on his priority list remained funding. He would have to re-engage with Stacy in the morning to see what the statuses of his requests were. If he got wind that Paul's requests were getting approved, at least he might have a leg to stand on when demanding more money be channeled to him. Secondly, he was placing the security interoperability firmly on Charlotte and Will's shoulders. He had meant what he said to Paul. He wasn't going to waste his time anymore getting into fights with Paul when he had countless other more important things to do. As far as he was concerned, Charlotte and Will could focus on playing nice while he focused on keeping the business online.

Thirdly and finally, he was going to have to try and get on Brandon's calendar. Whatever Paul had said today, Russell was sure it hadn't painted him and the IT staff in a positive light. If Russell didn't get out ahead of this, he could see some issues arising in the future. He wrote his list of three items on a sticky note and placed it on the top corner of his computer monitor. In the morning he would start trying to fix whatever damage Paul had done.

Chapter 13

Wednesday, 10 May

"Alright, what do you have?" Paul asked.

Across from him sat Bill, the lead on his strategic planning team. Paul was still surprised at how rapidly Stacy had been able to route funding to him. He had waited a few days after his meeting with Brandon in March before formalizing and submitting paperwork to Stacy. He had done the math on how many people he was requesting, the budget increase it would require, and the projected return that he would derive by having a strategic planning team. Still, he had expected it to get rejected or at the very least delayed for months. Instead, Stacy had come back less than a week later and told him to start interviewing for a team of five.

Bill had been the obvious choice to lead the team, coming from a consultancy where he had helped dozens of companies grapple with the same issues that Windward Financial Group was facing. Underneath him, Paul had inserted a team of four from various backgrounds, all focused on helping develop the strategy for Paul's entire staff.

"We've identified numerous things that need to be fixed and have begun drafting plans of action in accordance with Lisa's weekly working groups," Bill responded. "Most of it will require system changes and more in-depth work than we can do on our own. However, one of the biggest issues is the need to do a full review of user access rights and permissions. At least 20% of the accounts looked at in a random survey were operating above what their rights and privileges should have allowed and were able to access sensitive data outside their scope. Everyone is paranoid about who from the outside could attack us next, but my team feels strongly that one of the first things we need to look at is protecting us from internal harm, whether it's malicious or accidental."

"I thought Lisa and Charlotte's working group had already identified this issue?" Paul asked.

"You're absolutely right. They identified it in one of their earlier meetings and marked it as a high-priority item. However, their focus is understandably on the integration of security with the IT architecture right now. If they don't get that right, then they don't have a leg to stand on with the rest of the issues. This problem that I'm talking about is much broader than what those two are looking at. It's an enterprise-wide issue that will require an enterprise-wide approach. I suggest we not overload Lisa's team and instead spin off three of my staff to start doing the review. With the number of organizations in our company and the general amount of work that needs to be done, if we can get help from one or two IT guys, we should be able to knock it out in a month, assuming nothing crazy is discovered."

Paul paused and mulled over that for a few moments. "So, you think this is significant enough to warrant cutting more than half your team off to it for the next month?"

"Absolutely," Bill responded without hesitation. "I know you want us to take a more strategic approach so that you can determine how best to steer this ship, but if we don't take care of this issue then you're potentially steering a boat that already has the threat onboard."

"What is it with you and Lisa and these boating references..." Paul muttered.

Bill laughed. "I have no idea. I've never been on a boat myself, but they always seem to make the best analogies when discussing security and leadership issues."

"Alright," Paul said. "You mentioned that you would need IT support. What exactly do you need them to do for you?"

"Well, they're the ones who would ultimately help make all the alterations. We can develop the methodology and go through the review process, but I'd rather have them make the necessary changes so that we don't accidently impact other systems. They should have a good grasp on

database management and how user rights and privileges can be safely lowered."

"Okay, so you'll be doing most of the heavy lifting and they'll just need to be available to go through the motions of making the changes?" Paul asked.

"Exactly."

"Good. That shouldn't be a hard sell to Russell. His staff has been working around the clock lately, but I can't imagine that this would stress his personnel too hard. I'll bring it up at the meeting tomorrow with everyone. Before then, please have your team draft up a plan of action on this so that I can reference the key metrics and timelines we're looking at. This may disrupt some of the individual business operations, so I want to give the senior leadership enough time to prepare themselves before we come stomping in and editing rights. This is going to require a good bit of work and collaboration from all the business units. We can help with the review and work internally with IT to make the changes, but ultimately, it's the business units that own the accounts. They'll have to determine what their business requirements are before we go in and start changing everything."

"You know," Bill started hesitantly, "that the longer we let this be an issue, the more likely we are to have an issue?"

"I understand, and I'm willing to accept that risk. This issue has been one that has been around far longer than I care to admit. A few extra days is just something we'll have to manage. I have to consider the business requirements on this one. Whether or not they've been doing it on purpose, I guarantee some of the business owners have been using elevated permissions amongst their staff to streamline some of their processes. If we go in and take that capability away from them without giving them the opportunity to develop an alternative method, then we'll lose all support from the company. We must make these changes as transparent to everyone as possible. That means giving them the

opportunity to fix it themselves before we come in and fix it for them," Paul replied.

He continued, "Also, I'm going to reach out to Mitch and the other business leaders to ask them to have subject matter experts sit at the table with us to develop the roles and attributes for each user group. The reality is, they own the product and usage, and we are the custodians."

Bill nodded in agreement. "Got it. I'll have my team draft up what our plans are and when we plan on doing them. I'll have it for you this afternoon, so you have time to review it before tomorrow."

"Sounds good, Bill. I appreciate your team jumping on this. I know you've only been around for a few weeks, but you all are already proving to be an invaluable part of the team."

"Well, I appreciate that, Paul. And I'll be sure to pass along your words to the rest of my team."

Bill excused himself from Paul's office and left to go round up his team and get them started on drafting the access rights review plan. After he was gone, Paul opened his laptop back up and began typing up notes for tomorrow's meeting. He agreed with Bill's stance on the matter, but he also knew that Bill's team would be walking a fine line with this. There was no doubt in Paul's mind that at some point during the review, some business process would be interrupted when someone came to work one day with fewer permissions than they had the day before. It would have to be sold very carefully to the rest of the executive leadership or it would be dead before it even started.

In addition to that concern, Paul would have to figure out how to broach the subject with Russell. Paul had put on an optimistic tone with Bill, but the relationship between Paul and Russell was tenuous at best. The last few months had mended some of the issues, but Russell could still be hard to work with when it came to requesting any sort of manpower from him. Charlotte and Will had proven to be good inroads into the IT staff

during their weekly mee  _____ something
of this size and scope wc _____ Paul to engage directly with Russell.

A knock on his door distracted him from his thoughts. Lisa was standing in his doorway waiting patiently, most likely a side effect of her time with the government. The rest of Paul's staff just invited themselves into his office without waiting.

"Hey Lisa, just the person I wanted to see," Paul said, waving her in and motioning for her to take a seat.

"Oh yeah?" Lisa said, settling into the chair opposite Paul. "Only good news, I hope?"

"Maybe," Paul said. "Then again, maybe not. It'll all depend."

"That's awfully cryptic. What's up?" Lisa asked.

"At tomorrow morning's meeting I'll be unveiling Bill's team's next project. We're going to be running a complete review of access rights and privileges and bringing everyone back to the appropriate level."

"About time," Lisa cut in.

"Agreed. And I gave Bill my support to start getting ready. But tomorrow I'll be telling the rest of the company leadership that they need to take a hard look internally to see if they're compliant before Bill and his team come through. That's probably not going to be well received. People have had these elevated privileges for as long as I've been here and telling them that I'm finally getting around to fixing it is probably not going to make me any friends. That being said, I'll be introducing this as a collaboration since they are the users and the subject matter experts on who should have access, and how much."

Lisa leaned back in her chair and eyeballed the ceiling, probably working through the issue in her head. "Makes sense. So, what do you need from me to support this? Want me to grease the skids with Charlotte and her team?"

"No, I'll be going directly to Russell and Mitch about this. I want you to be an observer tomorrow. I'll be focused on delivering the news and won't have the chance to see everyone's reactions. I need you to just watch and see how people react to the news. Off the top of my head, I can promise you that Mitch isn't going to be a fan. He's used to getting whatever he wants, and I have no doubt that's in large part because some of his employees are doing things they shouldn't be able to do. I just want you to take in the reactions and let me know what you observed afterwards. That way I can approach this problem in the best way possible."

"Got it," Lisa said, looking oddly determined.

"Perfect. Now what did you stop by for?" Paul asked, leaning back in his chair and preparing for his latest update on the interactions between the security and IT managers.

Chapter 14

Brandon rambled on, talking about how prosperous the company was and how great the acquisition was looking. Lisa had stopped listening to details a good bit ago, recognizing the speech for what it was – a morale-building sales pitch. She had seen more than her fair share of military commanders stand in front of their subordinates and give the same sort of speech. It was intended to instill confidence, but after hearing so many of them, all it ever did to Lisa was instill a deep sense of boredom.

Lisa occupied herself by watching everyone else in the room. She figured it would help to develop a baseline so she could gauge reactions to Paul's upcoming announcement. Most of the senior leadership seemed to be paying rapt attention to every word Brandon said, including Paul, but occasionally Lisa caught her peers glancing around the room and doing the same thing she was doing.

She caught Charlotte's eye from across the room and shared a knowing smile before continuing her scan. Next to her, Paul continued to pay attention to Brandon, but Lisa caught him occasionally glancing at the notes in his lap, most likely trying to rehearse his announcement all the way up until the last moment. Lisa subtly put her hand on her leg closest to Paul and shot him a quick thumbs up, noting his small grin in return.

At the front of the room, Brandon appeared to be losing steam and trailed off, opening it up to questions and comments from the group. As usual, Mitch was the first one to speak, wanting to underscore his organization's strength and their readiness for the acquisition. One of these days, Lisa thought wryly to herself, she was going to be the first one to make a comment only to be able to watch Mitch's face. She caught Paul staring at her, frowning slightly but mirth showing in his eyes as though he could read her thoughts. Sometimes she worried he could. He had gotten much better at predicting not only her thoughts on particular issues, but other people's as well. Maria had joked the other day that someone should

register Paul as a psychic, seeing as he always seemed to have the answers to the questions he was asked, no matter how random they were.

After Mitch was done with his speech, the comments continued to go around the room with each executive feeling the need to at least say something, even if it offered no value to the conversation whatsoever. Surprisingly, when it got to Stacy, she kept it short and concise, making only a minor reference to the new budget system that had been in place for the last few months. Lisa had to respect Stacy; she had fought an uphill battle getting buy-in from the various business units, but now it seemed to be paying off as her new system better validated where money was being allocated. Besides, her new system had funded Bill's team, which was more than enough for Lisa to wholeheartedly approve it.

Finally, it was Paul's turn. He cleared his throat before beginning and glanced down at the papers in his lap one final time.

"In order for us to best support both the current business requirements as well as the future business needs, I've had a small strategic planning team begin conducting an analysis on what needs to be done to reduce risk," he began. "One of the things that were recommended, which I completely agree with, was a complete review of user account access rights and permissions. Over time, people have slowly had their permissions expanded, so that now we have people in this business capable of accessing and editing data that has absolutely nothing to do with their job requirements. I know nobody likes to think that someone on the inside may cause harm, and by no means am I trying to imply that we have malicious insiders within this company, but the way our current structure is set up leaves a lot of vulnerabilities and non-malicious mistakes that can easily be fixed through this review."

Lisa watched all the reactions in the room as Paul spoke. For the most part, everyone seemed to be paying attention. There were a few who Lisa

thought might be trying to stifle a yawn, but other than that, Paul seemed to at least be phrasing his comments in a way that kept the focus on him.

"I can't promise this will be a seamless transition," Paul continued. "Some of the accounts have had elevated permissions for months, if not years, and have likely come to expect and utilize the illegitimate access they have been granted. That's why I wanted to bring this up here before pushing forward with the plan. I wanted to give each of you a chance to prepare yourselves and your employees for the potential implications. Many of your staff have access to data they don't need to perform their assigned duties. We, all of us collectively, need to review this and ensure that we limit exposure. I just want to underscore the fact that this is a combined effort, with everyone having a critical role to play. The intent here is to ensure that we are not only compliant with regulatory and industry requirements, but also to enhance ease of planning and oversight in subsequent events. By creating roles, attributes, and key job indicators, we will make the selections, approvals, and reauthorizations much easier and less time-consuming in the coming years. If we put in the hard work now, this will ultimately lead to huge cost savings in the long term. What I'm asking of each and every leader is that you assign a subject matter expert to be part of the planning process. You own the product and are the experts in what each role does. This will allow for a more seamless and fault-tolerant cleanup process. Obviously, exceptions can be made, but those will be handled on a case-by-case basis by me and my staff."

"I love the idea of having a voice in this, but I can tell you right now, my staff is going to need some of those exceptions," Mitch interjected.

"That's perfectly fine," Paul replied, not appearing flustered at all by the interruption. "As I mentioned, they can be handled on a case-by-case basis. But just as with Stacy's program, my staff will need a clear explanation for why you want certain members of your staff to maintain elevated permissions."

Lisa expected Mitch to fight that but was surprised to see him nodding in understanding and leaning back in his chair instead, apparently content with Paul's response.

"Who exactly is going to be making these changes?" Russell asked.

"That's something you and I are going to need to talk about. I was hoping to catch you one –on-one before this, but we're admittedly going to need a little help with this. My team will be doing all the heavy lifting, but we're going to have to ask one or two of your people to implement the changes. We can discuss the details after this meeting."

Lisa watched Russell visibly struggle with his response.

"Yes. Let's," he finally responded, staring heatedly at Paul.

Lisa caught Charlotte's eye once again and gave her an inquisitive look. Charlotte replied with a small shrug, looking like she was just as confused at Russell's response as Lisa. There was a momentary silence in the room before Brandon cut in and asked if anyone else had any questions or comments. After a few other statements were made, the meeting mercifully came to an end and most people began filtering out. Russell, Lisa, Paul, and Charlotte all remained seated, waiting as people gathered their things. Brandon and Stacy were the last two to leave, casting glances at the four individuals that remained seated before making their way out into the hallway and closing the door behind them.

Paul and Russell both stood up and walked to the front of the room, while Lisa and Charlotte walked to the back of the room to give the CIO and CISO their space.

"What do you think that's all about?" Lisa whispered to Charlotte, nodding towards the front of the room where a heated conversation was already beginning.

"I honestly don't know," Charlotte said back in an equally quiet voice. "He's been extremely stressed lately about manning requirements and some of the infrastructure problems we've been having, but I still didn't

expect that sort of response. Between you and me, Paul's plan of action makes perfect sense to me. It's something that we've wanted to do for a while. In all reality, that may be what set Russell off. He may have wanted to be the one to propose that plan and move forward with it."

The voices coming from the front of the room weren't completely audible, but one voice was starting to get louder and louder. It clearly belonged to Russell. Lisa saw Charlotte noticeably cringe as she realized what was being said by her boss.

"I get that," Lisa replied, "but at some point, those two are going to have to get past their differences and learn to work together. You and I have a good working relationship, but that does us very little good if neither of our bosses can endorse it."

Charlotte rolled her eyes and nodded in agreement. "I'll try and talk him off the ledge. I'm sure I have one or two people I can spare to help out. At the very least, we can make it look as though this was a collaborative idea between our two staff. Maybe we can save a little face in front of the rest of the senior leadership."

"Just tell me what you need from me," Lisa said.

"I will. Let me talk to Will about it, and we'll try and come up with a plan on how to sell Russell on the idea. He gets heated up very quickly, but once he calms down, he's a lot more prone to accept recommendations," Charlotte replied.

Their conversation was interrupted as Russell stormed by them and out the door. Paul remained standing at the front of the room, clearly seething as he watched Russell disappear around the corner.

"Ladies," he said curtly, nodding at both Lisa and Charlotte before departing and heading in the opposite direction of Russell.

"I'm going to go see what all that was about," Lisa said, quickly gathering her stuff. "I'll shoot you an email later with an update from my end."

"I'll do the same," Charlotte said, letting out a large sigh before hurrying after Russell.

Lisa caught up with Paul halfway to his office and fell in stride beside him, remaining quiet. He glanced at her out of the corner of his eye and shook his head slightly.

"Let me calm down first," he said. "And then you and I can talk about what we're going to do."

Chapter 15

Monday, 15 May

Charlotte tried to hide her yawn as she trailed behind Will. She had spent most of her weekend drafting up various courses of actions for the projects her team was staffed on. She had meant to do most of them on Friday, but after last week's events she had spent all day Friday locked in a room with Will and some of the other managers, doing contingency planning. Russell had finally relented and given the green light to support the security staff, but he had put in place some stipulations that she was sure Lisa would be none too thrilled to hear.

Most of the other regular members of the weekly meeting were already in the conference room by the time Charlotte and Will arrived. Lisa and Maria were at the front of the room talking to some of their staff as Charlotte made her way to her regular seat towards the middle of the table.

"Charlotte. Can I snag you for a moment?" Lisa asked, nodding towards the back of the room and making her way there.

Charlotte set her coffee cup and notepad down in front of her chair and followed Lisa over to the corner, noting that Will and Maria were already talking on the opposite side of the room.

"What's up?" Charlotte asked as she drew nearer to Lisa.

"I wanted to talk with you first before it was announced to the room. I don't know what your plans are, but Paul intends to push forward with the review regardless of IT support. His goal is to create a comprehensive list of issues and accounts that need to be fixed. Whether or not Russell decides to act on it is a different issue entirely. I just didn't want you to feel like we were going behind your back on this. I think Paul is trying to make sure that in the event of an incident, the blame doesn't land in our laps."

"So instead, it will land in ours," Charlotte said, not intending for it to be an accusation but just following the logical progression.

Lisa paused and stuttered, "Well... that's not necessarily the intent..."

Charlotte held up a hand to silence her. "I'm not upset at what you're saying, Lisa. I'm just stating the facts. It makes complete sense from your point of view, and I can't fault you for that. But you and I both know that Paul understands the potential implications of his actions."

"I think he's just trying to solve an issue that he views as critical," Lisa replied.

"Well, lucky for the both of us, Russell finally came around to admitting that he viewed it as a critical condition as well," Charlotte said with a grin. "He's agreeing to cut off a section of my team to make the changes your team identifies. He just had one stipulation as far as how they would be utilized."

Lisa arched an eyebrow. "And that is?"

"He wants your team to complete the review before we start doing our piece. He doesn't want us to be working on this disjointedly, doing a small piece every day. Instead, he wants the changes to be comprehensive and done after you've identified all issues within the entire organization."

Lisa paused for a moment, tapping her chin with a finger. "That will delay solving the issue, you know."

"Right, but only for a few weeks. That will give us time to review the work you've done and develop a complete plan of action on how to implement the changes. It will impact the organization less and will also mean that our manpower won't be quite as overwhelmed. Plus, this has been an issue for a while; I don't think Russell minds having it take another few weeks to get fixed."

"Well, if that's what it takes to be able to utilize you guys, then I guess that's the plan. It's not ideal, but it's certainly better than nothing. Glad to hear we're at least moving in the right direction."

"Agreed," Charlotte replied.

"Alright," Lisa said, shifting the conversation topic. "I'm going to kick off this meeting. I'll open with what you and I decided on and then we can move forward to wargaming some of the other items on our list."

Charlotte nodded and made her way back to her seat, frowning slightly as she realized her coffee was no longer warm. Will slid into his chair next to her a few moments later, leaning over and asking, "How was your conversation?"

"Good," Charlotte replied in a low whisper. "She was smart enough to know that it was either this or nothing. Sounds like we'll be able to push forward with this without a lot of resistance. Yours? I saw you over there with Maria."

"Same general theme," Will said. "She didn't seem overly thrilled that we would be withholding our support until the end, but she also knew there probably wasn't going to be a better option anytime soon."

Both were interrupted as Lisa began speaking.

"Good morning, everyone. I hope you all had a good weekend. I figured we'd get the most critical piece of information out of the way early and then move to the ongoing projects from last week's meeting. As of this morning, both the security and IT staff have decided to move forward with the account review that was proposed last Thursday. The security staff can organize and facilitate the review of key entitlements in conjunction with the various business owners. We can provide recommendations based off some big data analysis to make sure the business units know what options are available to them. Once we've done our due diligence and worked with the business units to identify all the accounts that need to be altered across the enterprise, then an IT

section belonging to Charlotte will do a comprehensive review of our proposals and knock out all the changes in one pass."

"Doesn't that leave us vulnerable for longer?" someone Charlotte couldn't see on the security side of the room asked.

"It does. But not indefinitely. Also, it allows Charlotte's team to take a much more holistic view of the changes before they make them. I think that alone validates the potential vulnerability remaining for a few weeks longer," Lisa replied.

"Lisa, do you mind if I say something?" Charlotte said from her seat. Turning to address the rest of the room, she continued, "I understand that many of you are concerned about this issue not being resolved in a timely fashion. The intent on my end is to make sure we are making even changes across the board. Instead of slapping a bandage over certain issues, I would like to guarantee we solve the problem as opposed to the individual symptoms. We need to plan on how to carry this forward as an established process so that we aren't redoing this next year. In the end, my staff is going to have to balance security with business needs. We aren't trying to be difficult; we just have to view this from a different lens."

"You have our full support on this," Will said from beside her. "Once we have documentation listed out with the proposed changes that need to be made, we'll start digging into it immediately. That much I can promise."

There were nods from around the room as people agreed, and slowly they turned their attention back to Lisa. She made a few remarks on Charlotte and Will's comments and then moved on to more mundane tasks. Less than an hour later, the room was emptying out as people went back to their desks to get ready for the week ahead. Lisa mentioned that the security staff would be starting their review that afternoon and that she hoped to have a final product to present to the group in three weeks' time. Charlotte thought that timeline was a bit optimistic, but she didn't

say so. The faster she got the results from the security team, the faster she would be able to re-engage Russell about providing support.

Chapter 16

Monday, 22 May

As the group sat around the large conference room table, or joined in virtually to the meeting bridge, it was evident that they had a lot of work to do. Bill had pulled together as much information as possible over the course of a week. He then transposed it to a highly detailed set of spreadsheets as well as large poster board sheets plastered across all the walls. In fact, even the backs of the doors and all the pictures on the walls were covered in 2x4 poster board with various details, charts, numbers, and diagrams.

Each poster board contained information about the applications, systems, users, types of data, current business owners, how the apps or systems were used, and anything else he could get his hands on. Bill just hoped it was enough to get them started.

The security team members looked on with huge grins, thinking that they'd be able to easily show how bad the situation was and how they could solve it. The IT members sat with somewhat sullen faces, knowing the painstaking work it had taken to get this far and how much more would be required to get to a reasonable end goal.

The Business Unit subject matter experts were a completely different story, if their body language could be read correctly. Without exception, they were all looking around the room and back to their security counterparts; arms crossed defensively, frowns on every face, and seemingly concerned that this would be like every other security flaming hoop they'd have to jump through at the last minute because of some unknown threat or vulnerability.

As Bill started the meeting, he could see this was going to be a tremendous challenge, much more than just the security work that

needed to be done. They'd have to cross bridges to make sure they worked well together.

"Alright, everyone, thanks for joining today, we've been asked to get a handle on our RBAC and ABAC as quickly and efficiently as possible, but to be candid, I think we'll need to do this in several passes, looking at the most critical privileges first."

Ellen and John, both from Mitch's organization, had confused looks on their faces that Bill misinterpreted at first. He asked them both, "Did Mitch not tell you what the meeting was about and what we were here to do?"

Ellen spoke up first, "He did, but I have absolutely no clue what all the acronyms are you're throwing around. We were told to participate and help in making sure that our business users, customer service representatives, and management team had access to what they needed and that we don't take the business down by locking people out of things they need to perform their job."

Bill began to understand the confused look and stepped back a bit to explain.

"Okay, I think I can clear this up. RBAC and ABAC, the acronyms I mentioned earlier, are access control mechanisms that help define what people or systems should have access to in order to perform their job. RBAC refers to Role Based Access Control, essentially referring to the job someone performs that is just like all these other people and what they should be able to do in the system. ABAC is Attribute Based Access Control, really a macro set of RBAC, that looks at distinct attributes or things that make up the requirements, and grants or disallows access."

This time John beat Ellen and responded first. "Nope, didn't clear that up at all. I still don't get why we are here to work on this."

Maria thankfully chimed in quickly to help, "So, think of it this way, you're here because you know better than anyone else what a customer service

representative needs to do their job. Security and IT can pull all the data, understand what can be changed, and make the changes, but at the end of the day, you and our other business partners really know what it takes to do the job."

John and Ellen were stunned, as this was the first time they had heard security or IT acknowledge that they, as the customer, had a say in the process and could provide value. John responded, "Okay, so you're saying that we'll walk through all this stuff plastered over the walls and at some point, I'll understand it?"

Bill sighed and said, "I hope so. Let's get started!"

A few hours later there was palpable excitement and energy in the room as the teams worked together. The security team was beginning to understand the intricacies and challenges of the business with the different roles and the many exceptions. The Business team members were taken aback by the number of things to consider, but also the clear items that were problematic.

"Wait, wait, wait, you're telling me this customer service representative has the ability to order a service on behalf of our customer and approve it?" John asked in shock.

Ellen, trailing on John's concern said, "How do we fix that? They should never be allowed to approve an order. That's a managerial task. Hell, with what you're showing here, our CSRs could be defrauding us or our customers without us ever knowing it."

Bill smiled as the team was making progress and working well together. "It's even worse than that, since this is a direct Sarbanes-Oxley violation. The good news is that we can easily fix this now that we've identified it!"

Bill continued, "You can all see this is going to take several weeks for a company our size to get the basics and framework in place. Why don't we call it a day? I, for one, am feeling brain dead and need a break."

There was agreement around the room and on the meeting bridge from several tired voices, but the general feeling was positive now that they understood the problem, agreed to it, and had come to a level of collaboration.

Chapter 17

Paul blinked furiously, trying to clear the spots from his vision as he re-read the email for the third time. Sometimes he hated staring at a computer all day long. Today was no exception, as he tried to understand what Russell was trying to say. Bill's team had provided the IT staff with their final product almost two weeks earlier. So far, there hadn't been any movement on it from the IT side of the house. Paul had sent what he felt was a benign email to Russell, asking if his staff needed any help from Bill in understanding what the recommendations were. Russell had just shot Paul a response that essentially said the changes weren't going to be made any time soon since he was undermanned and he didn't see any justification to rush any of the "non-critical" recommendations Bill's team had provided.

Paul was just about to hit the reply button when his phone started ringing. Across the caller ID section, it listed "MITCH".

"Hey Mitch, what can I do for you?" Paul asked, picking the phone up and minimizing Russell's email so that he didn't have to look at it.

"Well, first I'd like you to tell me what the hell is going on," Mitch said, anger and frustration evident in his voice.

Paul immediately grabbed a piece of paper and pen from his desk drawer and replied, "Honestly, I don't know what you're talking about. Mind filling me in?"

"Yeah. All my business transactions and data were just wiped. That's what the hell I'm talking about. Are we under attack or what? This is completely unacceptable."

"Have you called IT yet?" Paul asked. "It's more than likely a computer or database issue. To my knowledge, none of our systems have identified anything that would be targeting your information."

"Of course I called IT. Russell had his staff investigat[...] / back saying that all the data from today's transact[...] According to Russell, we may not be able to recover it. [...] that?! I cannot afford to lose an entire day's worth of busi[...] of this, Paul. Russell told me it was probably a security issue, so [...] Now tell me, what the hell is going on?"

"Look, Mitch, I understand. I don't know what Russell was seeing that [...] not that led him to assume this was a security issue, but let me get with my team and try to get to the bottom of this. I'll send some members of my team over as quickly as possible so that they can start collecting the data we'll need to hopefully fix the issue. We should still have the incremental backups just in case we can't recover the original data. In the meantime, if you need anything else from me or my staff, or have any additional concerns, please don't hesitate to call back," Paul said, already typing an IM to Lisa telling her to come to his office.

"Sounds good, man," Mitch said. "Sorry if I'm coming off a little aggressive on this, but this is a major issue for my team."

"No worries at all, Mitch. That's what my staff is here for. Let me get together with them and give them a quick update on what's happening, and I should have someone over there immediately after. We'll figure this out. I'll give you a call back with updates as I get them on this end."

"Looking forward to it," Mitch replied before ending the call.

Lisa appeared at his office door a few minutes later, bringing Maria and some of her team leads with her.

"What's going on?" Lisa asked.

"Have we seen any indications of attacks that may have forced a data wipe of information belonging to Mitch's team?"

"Not that I'm aware of," Lisa replied. "Maria?"

e haven't seen anything like that," Maria said. "Why? Did something appen?"

"Mitch just called and informed me that he lost all business transaction data for the day. He said he called Russell's team and was told that the data was nowhere to be found."

"What makes him think this is an attack?" Lisa asked.

"IT told him that it was something that needed to be considered. I don't blame them. Everyone is just trying to get to the bottom of this," Paul said, choosing not to air his concerns with Russell with everyone in the room.

Lisa studied Paul for a moment, appearing to be reading between the lines before responding, "I'll dispatch a team over to IT to try and see if we can figure out what caused this. We probably won't be much help in the data recovery part, but at least we can do some root cause analysis and try to identify how this happened. We'll want to look at the data management and resiliency for recovery."

"I'll get the digital forensics team on this ASAP," Maria said. "Maybe it was just a user error."

"For it to be a wipe of this magnitude, it would have to be a very high-ranking user. But yes, both of you please go forward with those plans. I'm going to make a few calls to inform other entities to be on the lookout for data issues. Keep me posted on what you find."

After they had left, Paul began drafting an email to send out to the executive leadership. Before he could hit send though, his phone lit up again, this time displaying the name "BRANDON".

"This is Paul," he said, picking up the phone and typing the last sentence on his email, hitting send before Brandon started speaking.

"Paul, it's Brandon. I assume you're aware of the issue Mitch is having?"

"I am. My team is working with Russell and Mitch's teams to try and identify the cause of this thing. I'll be sure to let you know if it's a security-related incident. Right now, I don't have a lot to go off of, but this doesn't look or sound like an attack. I want to do some analysis before I voice my opinion, though. I told Mitch that we still have access to the incremental backups. I'm having someone investigate it now to make sure those are readily available and validated."

"Fair enough," Brandon said. "Look, Paul, I'm sure you understand that this is a very big deal. If we can't get to the bottom of this, it could have a significant impact. Every day of business is absolutely critical as we gear up for this acquisition and we can't afford to lose all the data on what was accomplished today."

"I understand," Paul said. "I'll keep you posted."

"Thanks," Brandon replied, hanging up the phone.

As soon as Paul had sat his phone down, it lit up for the third time, this time displaying "RUSSELL" on the caller ID.

"Hey Russell," Paul answered.

"Paul, I see Lisa is already over here so I'm sure you're tracking the issue. I'm almost positive this is a security issue, but I have my team working on this as well. We have an emergency meeting scheduled in an hour to talk about any discoveries. You and your crew are welcome to join."

Paul glanced at the clock and made a mental note of the time. "Thanks. I'm not seeing the same information that leads me to be confident this is an attack, but my team and I will definitely be there to discuss anything we find," he said emphatically.

Paul waited for a response but instead heard a click followed by the line going dead. He stared incredulously at the phone for a moment before setting it down and beginning to draft up another email to his internal staff to let them know about the meeting time and location.

The next hour passed uneventfully. Periodic updates from both Maria and Lisa identified some possibilities, but nothing definitively pointed towards a smoking gun. Paul printed off a copy of all the email correspondence relating to the issue and made his way towards Russell's conference room.

As he was rounding the final corner, Lisa suddenly appeared beside him, out of breath and looking a bit disheveled.

"I ran to your office, but you weren't there. Figured I'd catch you in the hallway," she got out, breathing heavily.

"What's going on?" Paul asked.

"We figured it out," Lisa said. "We looked through the logs of all activities that occurred directly before the data wipe and found what happened."

Paul glanced sideways at her, still walking slowly towards the conference room.

"An IT intern ran a script. According to Charlotte, he was hired by the IT team but loaned to Mitch to help his staff out. We don't know what his intent was, but it was most likely benign given the context. We think he was trying to erase a table in the database he was working on, and it just kept going."

"That doesn't make any sense. How could an intern be able to access the business databases that were wiped, let alone make any edits?" Paul asked.

"He ran it as an admin," Lisa responded.

Paul stopped and turned towards her. "How is that possible?"

"I honestly don't know. It looks like his account was flagged to have very stringent permissions, but somehow those rules were never put in place. He was able to run a script that could more or less do whatever it wanted."

"What have we done in response?" Paul asked.

"We froze his account and sent some people over to try and find him. Like I said, we don't think this was malicious. It looks like an accident. Either way, though, data recovery looks like a long shot at this point."

Paul paused to think about the implications of what he was hearing. "Is this something Bill's team identified in his findings?"

"Not this account specifically, no. The intern was hired only a week or so ago. However, it was noted that all new accounts needed to have their permissions established at creation, and that flagging them for future editing left us open to this sort of possibility," she said.

"Well, at least we identified it," Paul responded. "It's going to be hard to try and place the blame all on our shoulders for this."

"Is that really your biggest concern?" Lisa asked.

"Not at all. My biggest concern is the business right now. In all reality, where the blame falls shouldn't be a concern of mine at all right now. However, certain things have been, well, implied that have led me to think they may try to point the finger at us. At least now we have a leg to stand on," Paul said, noticing that more and more people were filling into the conference room. He started to make his way towards the door so that he could grab a seat.

"Agreed," Lisa said, falling in step beside him. "Although I think you're going to have a hell of a time convincing Russell of that."

Interstitial 2

As we've seen in the second part of this book, there has been a marked improvement in the level of business maturity and interaction seen by both Paul and the rest of the executive leadership regarding how security fits into supporting and enhancing the business. There has been a realization on both sides that while security is critical, and while there is a level of practicality in today's day and age, there are ways to prevent it from becoming an inhibitor. Communication between Paul and the executive leadership has evolved to the point that they are able to have an open dialogue about the current state of security. Paul has begun to understand, and thus educate others, that there will always be risk. The key to his emerging success is his ability to identify the appropriate, cost-effective, mitigation tactics and translate those into a business need.

This interaction with executive leadership has allowed him to start crucial and critical conversations between parties. Prior to this, the interaction was stressful and difficult. The executive leadership viewed Paul's perceived 'doom and gloom' mentality as fatalistic and unrealistic. When on the receiving end, Paul didn't initially listen to what was being asked and felt that he wasn't being given executive support. At the beginning, he wasn't thinking about the requests from a business

perspective; identifying costs, cost improvements, understanding ROI, and fully developed Key Performance Indicators (KPIs).

As he is evolving as a business leader, he has become able to define and articulate what the security organization needs are relative to the business drivers. Additionally, he is now able to better articulate the need for flexibility as security risks and regulatory aspects change at a rapid pace. This has provided a better foundation for him and the security team to build on with business collaboration.

As Paul has developed, his interaction with the IT department has evolved as well so that the common and basic security elements are being managed, maintained, and followed by the appropriate technical entities. This is the first step towards him creating a community of interest around security within the workplace. From here, the logical progression for Paul is to begin cross-collaboration with the rest of the business to develop a baseline level of understanding of basic security requirements and principles.

For years there have been reports and findings identifying that most breaches are the direct result of a gap in conducting security basics. These items include (but are certainly not limited to):

- **User training:** Phishing responses, sharing passwords, inappropriate

office use, lack of basic scrutiny with embedded links or attachments all create an entry point for malicious actions or inadvertently non-malicious mistakes.

- **Change management:** Not having full visibility and control over changes being made within the environment (including cloud resource) inhibits response and allows for mistakes.
- **Vulnerability management:** A core and fundamental area that should be at the forefront of a defensive posture. Patching known vulnerabilities in a timely manner, ensuring functionality and services that are unused are turned off and monitored.
- **Identity and Access Management (IAM or IdAM):** This is the primary goalkeeper – ensure that all entities (human, IoT, systematic, API, etc.) only have access to what is necessary to perform their function, with no elevated privileges. Maintaining multi-factor authentication to significantly reduce the success of malicious campaigns and limit the impact of non-malicious errors.

There are certainly many more fundamental areas to cover, but remember, the intent of the book is not to teach security basics, but rather how to take what the security professionals know and merge and meld them with the functioning business to improve and enhance the processes – NOT become a draconian barrier to success.

Before Paul, or any other security executive, becomes enamored with the most recent and flashy product offerings, an adherence to the basics is required. Basic blocking and tackling has proven time and time again to have the highest ROI for security departments. Of importance: going back to the basics does not mean an organization should forgo new techniques and tactics being created to combat developing threats. Instead, it means ensuring that very basic elements are not forgotten in pursuit of the latest and greatest technologies. This understanding is seen within the IT department at WFG to a limited extent. The IT department is already taking small steps towards covering down on these basic elements, but they are leaving the security department out of the communication channel. This miscommunication is the root of many of the issues that Paul experiences in the second part of this book.

The main gap that is identified is that there is a limited overarching, holistic, governance and compliance apparatus designed to handle the basics. Instead, it is an ad-hoc procedure thrown together by the IT

department that doesn't provide any metrics to measure against. A basic tenet of security, and an item that Paul has realized but hasn't been able to adequately articulate yet, is the concept that if you can't measure it, you can't see how well it's working. Paul recognizes this need at a very basic level and shows his attempt at correcting it by hiring Bill, but he is still very early into his discovery.

Simple but highly effective measures to help protect environments start with understanding, categorizing, and addressing risks head-on. While some new risks and threats do require specialized interaction and tooling, the majority do not. This process cannot, and should not, be viewed as a 100% solution. Rather, it is a foundation that recognizes that threats exist; tooling and resources may not. Once a threat type or vector is understood and categorized, the resulting action may be relatively simple.

The example in Part Two is a bit larger than most, but it's highly topical, as many organizations don't have a strong understanding of who has access to what data, systems, or applications, or at what level of access. Identity and Access Management, especially in the ever-expanding Internet of Things (IoT) area, is a highly complex and visible topic, but the basic steps are common in defining the risk and the resulting action plan.

The first step Paul takes is to assess the current situation and framework. After that, the team working the issue defines key risk

areas. Working with the business units, they collaborate to define correct attributes and, in further collaboration with IT and Business units, work to document and refine access entitlements. The actions do not require new tools. Instead, they require a collaborative work effort in defining the needs, developing new standards and policies that give a baseline level of oversight that was previously lacking. The Methods and Procedures (M&Ps) created give a more granular level of oversight that will hopefully become a living element holding the appropriate person or group responsible for the action/inaction.

Within WFG, there has been a similar maturation amongst the executives and the board. Their understanding of security is rudimentary at best, but their interest in the subject is growing. As the security representative to the board, it is Paul's responsibility to ensure their interest in the subject is fostered and not hindered. Additionally, he must remain tied into their concerns so he can either work to abate them or manage them. With their limited security experience, Brandon and the board are just as likely to be worried about the wrong things as they are to be worried about the right things. It is Paul's job to bring them to a level where they are not only capable of understanding his recommendations but also of making educated decisions based off what Paul and his team identify as issues.

As the news today overwhelmingly mentions security events, breaches, hacks, and

threats, executives are constantly bombarded with the risks, as well as a seemingly never-ending stream of companies offering the "magic fix" to all cyber-related issues. Executive responsibility in this area is to be aware, informed, and in communication with their security leaders to ensure the business, its assets, and its customers are protected against as much as possible within the capabilities of the business.

There should be a common understanding that hacks and breaches are not like what is portrayed by Hollywood but that they are rather proven techniques that are constantly revised and refined. As noted previously, these are mitigated in over 90% of the instances by basic activities and actions.

These can be as simple as and align with the previously noted fundamentals:

- Creating a manageable patch management process that does not allow known vulnerabilities to go unpatched;
- Ensuring that all users have the correct access to perform their job function, but nothing more;
- Encrypting data at rest and in transit;
- Turning off basic services that are not used to minimize threat vectors;
- Conducting asset inventories to know what assets should be connected to your network or

communicating with your applications/systems; and

- Conducting training and awareness programs to ensure that all employees are aware of the risks and their role in protecting the company.

There are many more common items that can be identified, but the key takeaway from this is that the executive team needs to be aware that they are not security experts (in most circumstances). They must find ways to effectively communicate concerns and objectives to enable and support the security organization as well as the ancillary supporting organizations, such as IT.

In the context of the story, Paul has begun to recognize how to effectively communicate with Brandon and the rest of the leadership. He must now find a way to use that newfound ability to provide focus, education, and clarity to the executive decision makers to ensure that he is able to guide the transformation of the security architecture.

PART THREE

Chapter 18

Monday, 19 June

"Paul! Come on in!" Mitch exclaimed, gesturing excitedly towards the small table in his office. He stood up from behind his desk and made his way towards the table as well, plopping himself into the seat opposite the one he had offered Paul.

"How are you doing today?" he asked, beaming as Paul took his seat.

"I'm doing well, Mitch, how are you doing?"

"Great!" Mitch replied, displaying in full force why he was such a good salesman as he gesticulated wildly. "We are absolutely crushing our numbers, in no small part because of your heroics !"

"I would hardly call what happened heroics," Paul replied with a smile. "Besides, I thought we had moved past that. I was just doing my job… nothing special about it."

Mitch waved his hand dismissively. "You see, man? That's your problem. You downplay your accomplishments, which leads others to subconsciously do the same. Your staff identified the issue and then managed to get everyone working towards a solution. That wasn't my crew, it certainly wasn't Russell's team – it was yours. Sell it, man. Be proud of it. Especially since it was my intern that created the problem, and your team identified it over a month ago to start looking at!"

"Trust me, I'm extremely proud of my team. However, the end goal is to prevent those issues from ever occurring at all as opposed to just becoming good at responding to them," Paul said.

"Baby steps, Paul. Baby steps. Just a few months ago nobody was giving a second thought to security. Now it seems to be one of the hot topics of the month. You're having an impact, whether you choose to admit it or not."

Mitch paused for a moment and then told Paul, "A mentor of mine once told me that you have a choice, you can either be a work horse or a show pony. You, my friend, are a work horse. You need to be the show pony occasionally to let others know all the great things you and the team are doing."

Paul let out a sigh and leaned back in his chair. "I'm not saying I'm not seeing the changes. I just need to find a way to make them faster and more comprehensive. I still feel as though my staff is primarily focused on fighting fires as opposed to getting out ahead of the threats."

"What threats?" Mitch asked, cocking his head to the side.

"What do you mean?" Paul asked, confused.

"I mean what threats are you trying to get out ahead of? And don't just give me the 'cyber threats' answer. Seriously, what specific threats are you trying to get out ahead of?"

"Cybercrime. Nation State attacks. Other APTs. New vulnerabilities that need to be patched. Ransomware. The list goes on."

Paul paused for a moment. "Creating a culture of security awareness so that employees don't accidentally or purposefully introduce threats that will have a legitimate impact on our business," he continued, wishing he didn't sound so defensive.

"Look, Paul, I'm not trying to put you on the spot or anything, I'm just trying to get you to look at this from a broader perspective. I'm not going to sit here and tell you how to do security, since quite frankly, I know next to nothing about. But what I can tell you is how to be successful in a business environment. Do you know why my team is so good at turning prospective clients into paying clients and then retaining them? It's not

because we all have charming personalities or are selling something the client can't get elsewhere. It's because before every single business transaction, we do an insane amount of analysis. The key is the fact that it's targeted analysis, not just analysis for the sake of crunching numbers. The most important thing we do is identify a need amongst our potential and current clients, and then work to tailor our offering to meet that need. Everything we do is tailored. There is no one-size-fits-all approach that works. Do you see what I mean?"

"I think I do, but by all means, please continue," Paul responded, wishing he had thought to bring pen and paper.

"I guess what I'm getting at is there's no way you're ever going to make our company one hundred percent secure, or at least, that's what you tell us. It's just like the fact that I'm never going to be able to have a one hundred percent success rate on every sales pitch my team does. But, with the right analysis and game plan going into it, we're able to stack the deck in our favor. The other business execs don't want to continually hear the sky is falling. They're much more comfortable sticking their heads in the sand and hoping for the best. However, if you can speak their language, you'll have their attention. You need to identify critical needs, which it sounds like you're working on, and then phrase it in a way that shows a solution coupled with a positive ROI. If you can do that, you're golden."

"That's the issue, though," Paul interjected. "I show that the investment produces a positive ROI, and it still gets kicked back. Yes we got some early headcount, but that was only to identify some of the issues"

"That's because you're looking at it from an accounting perspective. You're still thinking that if you can validate a positive ROI, regardless of size, then it's a worthwhile investment. The issue with that is it relies on the notion that we have unlimited resources. You need to be looking at this from an economics perspective. You and every other business unit owner in this company is competing for the same pot of gold, and every single one of them claims they can provide a positive ROI. In Brandon and

Stacy's mind, it comes down to who can create the biggest ROI with the funding requested. For instance, if we spend $200,000 on one of your projects, what's your validation for that?"

"I could easily use that funding to put better security measures on our customers' PII. That's my number-one priority. It would greatly reduce the risk of a breach and the leakage of customer data," Paul said.

"Okay, great," Mitch said, jotting down some notes on the paper in front of him. "So, you spend $200,000 on those security measures to reduce the risk of a breach. What's the current risk of a successful breach without those measures?"

"That's pretty difficult to answer," Paul replied with a frown.

"Just humor me. It doesn't have to be specific. Just a best guess."

"Well, given the rate at which our competitors are getting hit, I'd say it's about 20% per year that we get hit."

"Okay," Mitch said, jotting down the number 20 on the next line of his paper, "and with the new security measures?"

"It easily gets lowered to a single-digit percentage with the sort of protection I can afford with $200,000."

"Great!" Mitch said, putting a 1 down underneath the 20. "Now, theoretically speaking, if we experienced a breach, how much would it cost the organization?"

"Easily one million in recovery expenses," Paul responded. "But I've already done that math and provided it to Stacy. This isn't anything she hasn't heard yet."

Mitch nodded and set his pen down. "Right, but what you haven't taken into account is me."

"I beg your pardon?" Paul asked, perking up a bit.

"You need to look at this from Brandon and Stacy's perspective. You just told them that you need $200,000 to save them from a million-dollar breach that will occur roughly once every five years assuming your percentage doesn't fluctuate from year to year. That means you save the company $800,000 over the course of five years, or roughly $160,000 per year."

"That seems like a backwards way of looking at it," Paul said, watching Mitch write down the numbers on his paper.

"No, it's not. It's the way they look at it due to the fact that they have a finite number of resources to use. They don't see your security as an absolute investment because they know that if they give me that $200,000, I can create enough business to generate two million dollars over the course of the next five years. In that context, it's an easy decision for them."

Paul sat there frozen, at a loss for words. "How can that be?" he finally managed.

"It's all about changing the way you view the issue," Mitch said, setting his pen down. "You can't just show Stacy and Brandon that your investments will produce a positive ROI. You have to prove to them that you'll produce the best ROI with the funding requested."

"You make it sound so easy," Paul responded with a wry chuckle.

"I wish!" Mitch said. "Damn, if it were easy, then my life would be made. But it's not, which is why it's so incredibly difficult for companies to find individuals capable of doing it. At your level, you need to be less concerned with the ins and outs of security and more concerned with finding a way to enable and fund your managers. Instead of being so internally focused, you need to focus externally and allow your team to do their jobs. Right now, if I were you, my main focus would be on Stacy and the rest of the executive team. Convince them to believe in your team like you do, and I think you'll notice an incredible change of pace."

Paul leaned back in his chair and looked up at the ceiling deep in thought. Mitch had proven to be a great source of advice ever since they had narrowly avoided a disaster with the intern. Paul had been stopping by his office once or twice a week since then, talking about various aspects of the business. This wasn't the first time that Mitch had tried to offer advice, but it was the first time that he had been so direct about it. The truly interesting thing to Paul was the fact that everything Mitch was saying made perfect sense. The real question nagging at Paul was why he hadn't realized all this sooner.

"Are you still with me, buddy?" Mitch asked, smirking as he watched Paul get lost in thought.

"Yeah, sorry, just thinking about what you said," Paul said, snapping out of his thoughts.

"And...?" Mitch asked inquisitively.

"What you're saying makes perfect sense. I just feel like an ass for not realizing all this sooner. I've been so concentrated on the internal dynamics of my team that I failed to take a good hard look at the big picture. I've failed in being able to go external to the security organization and build out the relationships that are ultimately going to be necessary for success."

"Eh, don't feel like an ass," Mitch replied. "Do you know how long it took me to figure all of this out? I'll give you a hint. Way too damn long. And I'm a sales guy! The fact is you've already been moving in this direction. I have no doubt you would have figured all this out had you been given enough time. I'm just trying to speed it up a little for the sake of both the business and your sanity."

"Well, I appreciate you looking out for my sanity, at the very least. This is going to require some time to fully develop. I get the general idea and premise behind what you're saying, but actually producing the numbers and data is going to take a while."

Paul sat and contemplated, then continued, "The interesting part will be trying to put values and numbers around potential issues that won't drive revenue, but will incur residual perception and tension, even potentially in your area. The regulatory and compliance pieces are straightforward: you either comply or you get a fine and could lose operating licenses, credit issues, or other tangible impact."

"If it were fast and easy, everyone would be doing it. Hell, in your area, it's like selling insurance to an 18-year-old boy," Mitch said with a wink.

Paul had a confused look on his face, so Mitch elaborated, "Look, it's easy to sell life insurance to a family with a single-income, 45-year-old, overweight male with three kids. It's a given they need it. But try telling an 18-year-old boy he needs life insurance, and you'll have an impossible time making the sale. The question is 'why'?"

Paul began to understand the analogy and chimed in, "Because it's a given and self-explanatory for the family. I need to make the 18-year-old understand that there are funeral expenses, his debts, and other items that his family shouldn't be held accountable for."

"Bingo! Now, I think I've given you more than enough information for one day. You look like you could use some time to think, and I promised my wife I would meet her for lunch. Here's an easy ROI problem for you. Meet my wife for lunch and keep her happy or miss lunch and be terrified of going home tonight."

"Sounds like you better get going!" Paul said, standing and preparing to leave.

"You'll be fine, Paul," Mitch said from his seat. "You've already done tremendous things with your team and have gained the respect of the rest of the staff. Besides, if you're ever feeling down on yourself, just remember that at least you weren't the guy that named his company Pacific Group Finance when he works in the Midwest."

Paul froze in the doorway for a moment before bursting out laughing. "How have I never caught onto that before? Here I am, with their company name plastered on almost every piece of paper that crosses my desk, and I've never stopped to realize how ridiculous their name is."

"Welcome to the world of sales," Mitch said with a wink. "As long as the name sounds good, people will rarely question it."

Paul chuckled to himself as he turned and left, already thinking about some of the changes he was going to make once he got back to his office.

Chapter 19

"So... Anything exciting going on?" Tom asked, casually leaning back in his chair.

A flash of lightning momentarily distracted Brandon as he watched the rain pelt down the window behind Tom, leaving streaks running haphazardly towards the ground.

"Not much to report over this last month. Things still appear to be on track. Stacy has our budget under control and is projecting that we should still be well ahead of expectations. Aside from the small hiccup with Mitch, it was a relatively uneventful month, which is actually a great thing as far as I'm concerned," Brandon replied, still eyeballing the storm brewing outside.

"I heard rumblings about an issue a week or so ago," Tom said, leaning forward. "I'm assuming that's the hiccup you're referring to. From the sounds of it, your crew was able to recover everything before it became a major issue. Still, I'm intrigued, what exactly happened?"

"A, uh, an intern was able to compromise the database that housed Mitch's business, wiping all the data for the day," Brandon replied.

Tom arched an eyebrow and chuckled, drumming his fingers on the desk, "Well, that doesn't sound so good. What did you do with the intern?"

"We were able to identify that it was an accident. He had been doing some analysis on the data for one of Mitch's managers and accidently ran a script that wiped the data. In all reality, he shouldn't have been able to do as much damage as he did, but his account had elevated permissions, which is another issue entirely."

"So, if he wiped all the data, how were you able to recover it?" Tom asked.

"Paul recommended a while ago that we put in a robust recovery program both on site and in the cloud in order to conduct rollbacks in the event of data loss or data corruption. Admittedly, the staff dragged their feet on implementing it, but thankfully it had already been established prior to this event," Brandon replied.

"Sounds like good foresight on Paul's part. Just to play the devil's advocate with this, what would have happened had you not had the backup?"

"I don't have the exact figures," Brandon replied carefully. "But based on what Mitch, Paul, and Russell, all told me, it would not have been pretty. We used to back up our data in the middle of the night, and this was done towards the end of the business day. We could have potentially lost up to a day's worth of business. At the very least, the manual recovery process would have required a large pool of emergency resources."

Tom nodded absentmindedly, appearing to notice the storm outside for the first time. Brandon sat there quietly, wishing he were anywhere else. He wouldn't say he enjoyed every one of his one-on-one meetings with Tom, although he had to begrudgingly admit they were often beneficial. Still, Tom had the ability to get to the root of a problem faster than anyone Brandon had ever worked with, and it often led to moments like this, where Brandon knew he would be answering tough questions.

"So," Tom said, still staring out the window. "You had an intern run a script that he shouldn't have been able to run, wiping sensitive data, and by happy circumstances your CISO was smart enough to do his job and ensure that a situation like this wouldn't be a showstopper. I guess the only question that matters at this point is, what are you doing to make sure it doesn't happen again?"

"Paul's team had actually started working on a solution before this event even occurred; he just wasn't able to get it fully implemented in time. Since then, Paul, Russell, and Mitch have worked overtime to put in place a full review of accounts to ensure that people can't accidentally exceed their permissions," Brandon replied.

"That's a good start. Obviously, those changes should at least prevent a duplicate of this issue. However, have you considered the deeper implications of what happened?" Tom asked, pivoting so that he was once again fully facing Brandon, a slight frown evident on the corners of his mouth.

"I'm not sure I'm following you," Brandon said after a slight hesitation.

"All of your business units are proactive except the ones dealing with your IT infrastructure. Mitch is leaning so far forward on his projects I'm surprised his nose isn't touching the ground. Stacy has been highly proactive in all her endeavors, changing the budgeting culture *before* it was an issue. In fact, I think you'd be hard pressed to identify any of your business units that aren't ahead of the curve, except the issues pertaining to IT. I'm glad to hear you were already working on the permissions issue when this event happened, that shows you're on the right track, but your guys are still being way too reactive with security and IT. You need to find a way to make them more proactive, like the rest of your business. Instead of slapping a bandage on the issues when they arise, you need to be building a system that prevents the issues from occurring in the first place."

"I see what you're getting at," Brandon replied, "but I honestly don't know if it's even possible to be completely secure."

"Yeah, yeah, yeah," Tom interjected, cutting Brandon off, "I get it. Security isn't foolproof. I've heard the sales pitches and doomsday prophecies just like you have. I'm not saying you need to find a way to prevent all attacks, and I'm certainly not saying I'm a security expert, but right now it seems like you're still being way too reactive. You're moving in the right direction, there's no doubt in anyone's mind that you've shown significant growth in that area over the past few months, but you still have a way to go. It's a cultural issue at this point, and love it or hate it, that starts with you."

"I gave Paul the funding he requested for his new team of security analysts. So far, I've been nothing but impressed with what they've been

able to identify. Like you said, I think we're on the right track," Brandon said.

"You're making excuses right now," Tom said, a small grin forming on his face. "You gave your security and IT staff the resources to do their jobs, so now it's time to hold them accountable. Paul told you what he needed and promised you results. It sounds like he's trying to hold up his end of the bargain, but it also sounds like he may still need a bit of guidance on how his results nest with the entirety of the business. He's working too closely with Russell in isolation. He needs to view the business from all the other perspectives… only then will security transition from being a liability to an asset for you."

"I agree wholeheartedly," Brandon said, smiling for the first time. "Mitch beat you to that point. He identified it as an issue immediately after we recovered the data earlier this month. From what I've heard, Mitch has been going out of his way to help show Paul how his part of the business operates, so that Paul is able to make more educated decisions."

"I knew I liked Mitch," Tom said, returning the smile. "I would work to foster that relationship. Paul obviously wants to do the right thing, but he doesn't have all the tools he needs… yet."

"I think the more he experiences the rest of the business, the more he'll be able to identify the best ways he can help," Brandon replied, taking the lead. "The issue isn't his abilities, it's that he's viewing everything from a security perspective alone, without fully understanding the broader implications. The more he interacts with the other business units, the more likely he is to become proactive."

"Exactly!" Tom exclaimed, slapping his open palm down the desk.

"You know…" Tom added, a mischievous twinkle in his eye, "I think it's telling how much time we spend discussing security at these things lately. It seems like less than a year ago we wouldn't have even been able to spell security without a dictionary. Perhaps you should think about

bringing Paul to one of these things in the future. We spend so much time talking about him it might be helpful to have him share his thoughts."

"I'll be sure to bring him along in the next few months," Brandon agreed. "At the very least, it might be good for him to see what's being discussed at the strategic level."

Tom snorted in response. "Is that what this is? A 'strategic discussion'?" he asked, making the air quotes with his fingers. "And here I was thinking this was just a way for me to get out of the house occasionally."

Brandon couldn't help it and laughed out loud in response.

"Well, for the sake of appearances, maybe we shouldn't tell anyone that that's the real driving reason behind these meetings. Let them still believe that we're doing this for all the right reasons and whatnot."

"Agreed," Tom said, smiling. "Now, what else do you want to talk about?"

Chapter 20

"All I'm saying is there needs to be some form of expectation management in this place," Russell continued. "You and I need to be singing the same song tomorrow morning in order to fully make that point."

Paul tried to appear as though he was actively listening, but Russell had been ranting for well over the past ten minutes, and as the seconds wore on, Paul was finding it increasingly difficult to stay engaged.

"Does all of that make sense to you?" Russell finally concluded.

"It does," Paul began. "But I honestly don't think it's our position to be telling the business leadership how to handle this acquisition. As you said a few months ago, this thing is happening one way or another and it's simply our job to make it successful. I think that still holds true, despite the workload it's requiring."

"Right, but that comment was made before all of these issues began to arise," Russell shot back. "There was no way to predict there would be this many problems with integrating all the systems. Now that we're here, I feel like it's our responsibility to inform the company."

"I don't disagree with you there. We need to inform Brandon and the rest of the business leaders that there may be some issues. However, the decision to accept that risk and push forward is ultimately up to him. The best thing we can do is present it in a readily understood manner that he can make the decision with as much information as possible," Paul replied.

"So, you're not going to support me tomorrow morning," Russell said flatly.

"That's not at all what I'm getting at," Paul responded, actively trying to contain his frustration. "I just feel like there's a tactful way to approach this and then there's the way you're proposing. If we go in there saying that it can't be done without offering any alternatives, then we're going to lose all support. We can't just identify the problem; we also need to identify a series of solutions for the leadership to choose from and then make a recommendation. Brandon trusts us to lead these components of his company. It's our job to guide him towards the right solution."

"There are no solutions! That's the damn problem!" Russell said, turning red at the face. "At the current manpower I have, it simply can't be done in the time provided. The execution date needs to be moved to the right or we're going to cause a whole lot more issues than we're prepared to handle."

"What exactly is giving you the most concern?" Paul asked, reaching into his desk drawer to grab a pen and paper.

Russel hesitated, eyeballing Paul before replying. "Everything is a concern at this point. If I had to qualify that statement, though, it comes down to two main issues. We need to bolster our hardware to support the new business infrastructure, but we also need to format a lot of data in order to make the transition as seamless as possible. With all the competing requirements my staff is having to manage, formatting all the data is proving to be the straw that broke the camel's back. It's just too much right now."

"Okay, what if my staff was able to take on the data transformation piece to alleviate some of the workload on your staff. Would that be enough to keep us on track?" Paul asked.

"It should be. Assuming no issues arise from your staff, that should free me and my team up enough to handle the rest of the workload. Are you saying you're capable of doing that?"

"It won't necessarily be pretty," Paul replied, jotting down a quick note on his paper. "But, at the very least we should be able to support it. I'll

just need Lisa and Maria to get all the details about what needs to be done. They should be able to take it from there."

"I'll have Charlotte and Will prepare some notes to hand over. It shouldn't be too complicated; it just takes more man hours than I have to spare right now," Russell said.

"Sounds good. Are you still planning on bringing this up at tomorrow's meeting?" Paul asked, already knowing the answer.

"I don't see the need to at this point. You and I solved the problem internally, no sense in letting everyone else know about the issue," Russell said, rising from his seat, evidently deciding the meeting was at an end.

Paul simply nodded in response, writing a few more notes on his paper as Russell exited his office. After Paul heard his office door close, he set his pen down and leaned back in his chair, letting out a frustrated sigh. Of course, Russell didn't want everyone else to know that he had pawned work off on Paul. For a moment, Paul wondered if that had been Russell's plan the entire time. Tell a sob story, knowing that Paul would eventually offer to help as opposed to interfere with the business. Paul shook his head, realizing there was no sense in dwelling on it. He had offered his services and now he was on the hook for it. He typed a quick note to Lisa and scrolled through some of his emails while he waited.

She eventually appeared at his office door, pausing in the doorway just long enough for him to acknowledge her before coming in and taking her regular seat.

"You wanted to see me?" she asked.

"Yeah. So, I just had a … productive meeting with Russell, if you will," Paul said, trying to find the right words.

Lisa rolled her eyes. "That sounds riveting. What did you two discuss?"

"Oh, you know, the usual. His overwhelming workload coupled with the fact that he's the only one keeping this business together."

"I see," Lisa replied. "And I can only assume something important was decided or else you wouldn't have brought me here."

Paul chuckled wryly and slid his note paper across the desk to her. "He says with his current manning and requirements, there's no way he'll be able to handle the data formatting that's required for the upcoming acquisition. Instead of him going before the rest of the executive leadership and making an ass out of himself, I offered to help. It's not really our lane at all, but I figured it couldn't hurt to pick up a relatively easy task and earn some good graces in the process."

Lisa quickly scanned over the note paper before responding, "Did he ever stop to consider that we're overwhelmed as well before asking you to take on his job responsibility?"

"He didn't outright ask," Paul said. "Although the more I think about it, the more I'm convinced that this was his ultimate goal coming here. Still, at the end of the day, I volunteered to do it. We're not so pressed with competing requirements that we can't handle it. All I ask of you is that if any issues arise during this, you inform me immediately. I don't want us to say we'll help do something and then drop the ball."

Lisa nodded slowly. "Makes sense. If I'm honest with you, I'm not a huge fan of this. It isn't an overly hard task, but it isn't the easiest one either. There are a lot of things that could bog this down and make it far more time-intensive than I think we can handle. I'll get my team working on it, but I can't justifiably give you a proposed deadline just yet."

"I understand, and I don't expect one from you right now. I know this is getting tossed on your plate at the last minute. All I ask is that you collaborate with Charlotte and Will and get working on it as soon as possible. If you run into any issues that make this more of a project than I expected, let me know and I'll work to get Russell actively involved again."

"Good luck with that," Lisa said, grimacing.

"Yeah, well, at the end of the day, it's his responsibility. Either he can help us work towards a solution or he can tell Brandon why he's not going to be ready for the acquisition. Either way, it's not a major concern of mine. We'll help out where we can and leave Russell to figure out the rest. Our primary job is security, and that will take priority. This side project will just have to fit in where it can," Paul replied.

"Got it," Lisa said, making a small notation at the bottom of the note paper Paul had given her. "I'll get my team looking at it this afternoon and I'll talk to Charlotte and Will on Monday. We should be able to start coming up with a plan of action by this time next week."

"Perfect. There's one more thing I wanted to discuss with you, but I want Maria and Bill here for it as well," Paul responded, typing a quick note to those two.

"Care to give me a spoiler while we wait?" Lisa asked.

"Let's just say I had an interesting conversation with Mitch yesterday. I spent all last night thinking about it, and I think I finally see a way to get us the funding we need. It will require some reframing of our goals and objectives, but it should be able to gain a lot more traction with Stacy."

Lisa grinned from ear to ear. "I'm definitely looking forward to hearing this."

Chapter 21

Monday, 10 July

"Paul! Great to see you again! How have you been doing since the last time we spoke?" Tom asked, practically beaming as he led Paul and Brandon into the conference room.

"Things have been going really well," Paul replied, choosing to leave out the fact that the only time he had spoken to Tom before was during his hiring. "My wife and I are finally settling into our new house. On the work front, I think my team is making some good headway and getting the ball rolling on a lot of security initiatives."

"So I've been told," Tom said, settling down into his chair. "Also, I'd like to personally thank you for the work you and your team did on the data issue that occurred a couple weeks ago. From the sounds of it, your team saved the day."

"It was nothing," Paul said, feeling a little shocked that Tom knew about the role his team had played.

"That's not what Brandon says. He says your foresight allowed for policies to be developed that made the recovery possible. Without the work your team did, we might have lost a substantial amount of capital. That's hardly 'nothing' in my book."

"Tom and I discussed what happened during one of our last meetings," Brandon interjected, apparently sensing Paul's confusion.

"Well, I appreciate the vote of confidence," Paul responded. "I'd like to think that it was a team effort that enabled us to recover so quickly. I was just doing my job."

"Humble too, huh? You're a modern-day security superhero, aren't you?" Tom asked, laughing aloud at his own joke while Brandon and Paul glanced sideways at each other.

"Alright," Tom continued. "Down to business. Paul, the reason I asked Brandon to bring you along today is that I wanted to hear your thoughts on some issues directly from you. Many other boards and companies are still attempting to ignore security Issues by sticking their heads in the sand. I fully intend to tackle the issue head-on. You're our security expert, so I'm hoping to leverage your expertise to bring the entirety of the board up to a reasonable level of education on security. For now, though, I wanted to keep our initial meeting small so that we could speak candidly."

"Fair enough. What specifically do you want to talk about?" Paul asked.

"Let's start with how you think we are currently postured regarding security," Tom said, leaning forward in his chair and staring intently at Paul.

Paul paused for a few moments and formulated his thoughts before launching into his answer.

"Right now, I think we are reasonably well off. Over the years, the team has done a good job of implementing security measures against developing threats. However, those solutions were often made in isolation and don't play well with the other items. We have a lot of systems and processes doing things without speaking to the rest of the enterprise. It works for now, but it's not efficient and it opens us up to miscommunication and letting things slip through the cracks.

"I don't think it's a dire situation, but it's definitely something that is not going to get better on its own with time. Up until recently, there doesn't seem to have been an underlying strategy regarding the implementation of solutions. As such, it's more of a tangled mess of systems than a coherent, easily navigable solution set."

Tom tapped his chin thoughtfully as he listened to Paul. "And that's what you want to fix first?"

"I think that's what we need to fix first, yes. Like I said, we seem to be relatively secure for now, so instead of throwing new products at the problem, I think it would be much more prudent to reevaluate what we are currently using and see if there's a way to shape it into a more cohesive security environment."

"So, what's stopping you?" Tom asked.

"Honestly? I think one of the biggest hindrances is the budget," Paul said, glancing at Brandon to gauge his reaction to that comment. "I don't think we're being shortchanged necessarily, but this upcoming acquisition has everyone hurting for money. Second to that is the issue of unplanned work. I'm trying to develop workflow processes to handle it, but it continually seems to pop up at the worst possible moments."

Tom perked up at that. "Have you read *The Phoenix Project*?"

Paul paused and studied Tom. "Uh, yes. I'm surprised you've heard of it."

"A CIO buddy of mine at another company recommended it a few months ago. I read it while on vacation," Tom said, flipping his hand as though it wasn't a big deal.

"What's *The Phoenix Project*?" Brandon asked, speaking for the first time.

"It's a book on DevOps, IT systems, and processes," Paul said. "One of the biggest points the book makes is how to handle the different types of work that come up in a typical workplace."

"Huh," Brandon said, nodding his head slightly. "I wonder if Russell has read that book as well."

"I think everyone at this table knows the answer to that," Tom said offhandedly, catching Paul off guard.

"I'll have to check it out," Brandon said, either not catching on to what Tom had said or choosing to ignore it.

"Alright," Tom continued. "So, you want to develop a strategy that will hopefully eliminate ineffective or redundant systems and make the security apparatus much more effective. Your two hindrances are money, which is admittedly tight right now, and competing work requirements. What's your proposed solution?"

"I've got a list of proposals in front of Stacy right now. I'm hoping to hear back in the next week or so on whether we'll be able to move forward with some of them. Essentially, I want to bring proven systems onboard that will allow us to consolidate even further and get rid of ineffective systems, like you mentioned. I already have a team developing the strategy piece, so that as we bring these new systems into the environment, they can be tracked and provide us with a good picture of what processes we are running in specific situations."

"Sounds like you're on top of it," Tom replied. "How are you validating your ROI for these requests?"

"I do it in two ways and provide both of those to Stacy and her team. The first way is in a vacuum where I list all budgetary requirements and compare them against the returns we'll see by making these purchases. The second way takes that and expands it out into a more holistic view, comparing the positive ROI to the rest of the business. That way I can validate that it's not just a good security expenditure, but that it's a good business expenditure as well."

"I've been watching Paul's requests come across my desk," Brandon said after Paul was done. "He's getting far more effective at making his case, and obviously myself and Stacy are becoming far more aware of the security requirements of our company. A lot of the proposals Paul is mentioning should be able to find funding from somewhere."

Brandon then continued with another thought. "Another item that is helping significantly is the level and type of communication that is sent out from Paul or his team when issues occur. I've been getting positive feedback from the entire Senior Leadership team on this. I remember some of our earlier security incidents and we all felt like we were walking

in the dark. Now they are released quickly as short updates with clear information. It's really providing a level of confidence in your team, Paul!"

"That's good to hear," Tom replied, nodding his head in apparent satisfaction with the answer. "Speaking of funding, how is Mitch's team doing with the upcoming acquisition?"

For the next hour, Tom and Brandon went back and forth on details pertaining to other aspects of the business, allowing Paul to observe the conversation. Some of the projects they discussed were things Paul had never heard of before and had no idea WFG was pursuing. In the course of the hour, Paul realized how limited his knowledge still was of the rest of the business. Still, he walked out of the meeting feeling far more confident than he had been walking in and was already shooting off an email to Lisa by the time he made it to his car.

Chapter 22

Tuesday, 11 July

Stacy looked down at the paperwork in front of her, mulling over the data. Paul's latest budget requests were fairly detailed, tying a requested expense with a specific business need and displaying an organized ROI proposal. Most of his requests had endorsements from the various business owners, which meant Stacy would be hard pressed to do anything but approve the measures. Additionally, he had included a separate sheet in each of his requests identifying why his projected outcome was beneficial for the entirety of the business and how it was projected to outmatch other business unit requirements. His numbers were a bit off in her opinion, but there was no denying that he made valid points when it came to the criticality of some of the requests he was making.

Reaching across her desk, she grabbed her phone and punched in Paul's number, listening to it ring twice before he picked up.

"Hey Paul, it's Stacy. I'm looking at your budget requests and I was wondering if you could stop by when you get a chance?"

"Sure thing, Stacy. I'm on your side of the building right now, leaving a meeting with Mitch. Does five minutes work for you?"

"Sounds great, Paul," she replied, hanging up the phone and organizing the papers in front of her.

True to his word, Paul came round the corner and made his way towards her office about five minutes after she had hung up. Stacy noticed he was carrying a notepad in his hand and realized that he would have had no time to go back to his office and still make it here in five minutes. Whatever he had been meeting with Mitch about, he had evidently expected to take notes.

"Hey Paul, how's it going? I appreciate you doing this on such short notice," she said, rising to greet him.

"No worries at all! You mentioned it was about my reports. I hope everything is alright with them?" he replied, smiling warmly.

"Of course, of course. Please, take a seat. I just wanted to talk to you in person about some of the requests you submitted."

Paul slid into the chair across the desk from her and flipped his notepad open to a blank page, placing it on the corner of the desk in front of him.

"Alright," he said. "What did you want to talk about?"

"I wanted to discuss your requests. First of all, they're very good. What I wanted to talk about was the deeper motivation behind them. These are all individual requests for various parts of the business, and I wanted to know if there was some deeper strategy at work here."

Paul smiled broadly in response and leaned back in his chair, relaxing visibly. "As a matter of fact, there is. At the end of the day, my number-one goal is to enable businesses to be successful. Subset to that, my role is to keep the business secure and safe so that the various business units can drive revenue and enable our growth. My goal with all of those," he continued, gesturing at the sheets of paper in front of Stacy, "is to drive that point home. In each of those cases, the number-one concern is transparency. I went to each of the various business unit owners and discussed their needs and requirements. Those requests are nested with the requirements they indicated but are designed to slow down the system as little as possible. They are a touch more expensive than some other alternatives, but they have the benefit of not impacting the business processes they interact with at all."

"I see you included that logic in your proposed ROI," Stacy said, shuffling through some of the papers.

"I did. The way I see it, security ROI can be defined in multiple ways. First and foremost is the proposed cost of implementing the security measure

vice the cost of the data it's protecting. However, coupled with that is also an understanding of how at risk the data it's protecting truly is. I tried to outline all those numbers in the first column that I labeled "true ROI". Under the second column labeled "perceived ROI", I also included the statistics relating to how the security measures would impact the various business units. The more of an impact they had, the lower the ROI was. Good security measures should be as transparent and non-intrusive to the users as possible. Taking both the true ROI and the perceived ROI, I came up with the list of requests you see on my list. Each of them protects a critical component of the business units, whether it's customer data or proprietary information, while still enabling the business to operate unhindered." Paul paused at the end of his speech and looked at Stacy expectantly.

Stacy tried not to gawk at Paul. Where was all this coming from? Just a few short months ago, he had been sitting in her office asking her how she defined ROI. Now he was sitting here defining it for her in order to justify his budgetary requests.

"That sounds great, Paul. But if asked by a non-financial person, do you have a response prepared that they can understand as well?"

"Sure," Paul said. "At the end of the day, it comes back to identifying all costs associated with taking an action and comparing them to all costs associated with not taking it. When it comes to security, there are a lot of hidden costs in the mix as well as a lot of hidden benefits. What I've tried to do here is outline each of those costs in context as well as provide a key indication of why the hidden costs are greatly outnumbered by the tangible benefits."

Stacy sat there stunned, not sure what to say in response to Paul's answer.

As though he could read her mind, Paul smiled sheepishly and said, "I've had a good bit of help from Mitch getting to this point. My team came up with the numbers in front of you, but he's the one who got me on the right track."

"Well, whoever or whatever is responsible for it, this is really good work, Paul," she replied. "I can't promise everything will be approved because I haven't had time to crunch all the numbers yet. But these requests are exactly what my team needs to make the right decisions. From the sound of it, they nest nicely with the overall business goals, which means they should stand up to scrutiny."

Paul was beaming. "That's great to hear. All of that admittedly took a lot more work than I was expecting, but it's good to get the validation directly from you. No worries if you can't approve all of it, my team is already working to identify other concerns. Just so you're aware, the end goal for us is to streamline everything into a clear and concise strategy, which should ultimately result in cost savings. We'll have to spend money to get to that point, but the hope is to end up with a series of security measures that work in tandem with each other, allowing us to start getting rid of some of the superfluous and redundant measures we currently spend money on."

"Is that mentioned and quantified at some point in these requests?" Stacy asked.

"Not yet. I wanted to have it in there, but I couldn't justifiably put any numbers down. At this point, it would all be speculation and educated guessing. We aren't quite at the point where we can accurately identify what could eventually be cut. I just wanted to let you know that that was our eventual goal. Sooner or later Bill's team should be able to quantify that statement with some key metrics that I'll include in future budget requests."

"Makes sense," Stacy said, jotting down a note on one of the requests to remind her of this conversation. "I appreciate the honesty with that. You'd be surprised how many people try to just make up the numbers and then can't support them when questioned. I look forward to seeing what you and Bill are eventually able to present. For now, I was mostly concerned with making sure there was a strategy tying all these spending requests together. From the sounds of it, you've done your homework

and have gotten the support from most of the business leadership. Brandon will be interested in seeing this as well, so I'll be sure to bring it along with me to our next meeting. Speaking of Brandon, how did your meeting with him and Tom go yesterday?"

"It went really well, actually. We spoke about security for the first fifteen minutes or so. I was surprised by some of Tom's questions; he seems to have a good grasp of security. After that, the two of them went on to discuss other business issues for the next hour and a half. It was extremely educational to see what type of information was discussed between the two of them. It definitely served to further validate some of the changes I've been making amongst my staff to get them further integrated into the rest of the business."

Stacy nodded. "Tom is surprising like that. When I first met him, he grilled me for over an hour on various financial laws and regulations. At first, I thought he must have had a banker's background, but after asking around, I found out that he has been a serial entrepreneur all of his life. He just has an incredible ability to understand complex topics and break them down to their most fundamental forms. I'm glad to hear you found the experience worthwhile."

"It most definitely was. Now, I hate to do this, but Russell should be coming over to my office in the next few minutes and I have a few things I need to discuss with him. Was there anything else you wanted to talk about before I go?"

"No, that was it," Stacy said. "I appreciate you stopping by, and I'll let you know as soon as a decision has been made on your requests."

"Much appreciated," Paul said, rising from his chair and grabbing his notebook before departing.

Chapter 23

"What's going on, everyone?" Will exclaimed, walking into the conference room grinning. Charlotte followed closely behind, gripping her coffee cup and wincing at Will's loud voice. Lisa couldn't help but chuckle at the pair of them. She knew that Russell had been working both to the bone, and that Will's outgoing personality was just a cover-up for how exhausted he was. Everyone in the room was exhausted. The IT staff had been working nonstop to try and get all the systems ready for the upcoming acquisition, and the security staff had been working diligently to continue their day jobs, help the IT staff out where they could, and do the analysis on the numbers that Paul needed to pitch to Stacy.

At least on that front everything appeared to be going well. Paul had come back from his meeting with Stacy the week prior talking excitedly about the compliments she had paid him. As was his way, Paul was quick to identify that he hadn't done anything special and that instead it had been completely due to the hard work of Lisa, Bill, and Maria's teams. Lisa wasn't as confident as Paul that the funding would be approved, but she was interested in seeing if all that extra analytical work he had made her do would pay off.

"Quiet down, Will. Charlotte looks like she wants to stab you," Maria laughed, walking forward to shake his hand.

In response, Charlotte just shrugged in noncommittal agreement and made her way to her usual seat.

"How are you doing?" Lisa asked as Charlotte drew near.

"Oh, you know, same as the past few weeks. I hate to sound like a broken record, but the work requirements keep stacking up with no end in sight," Charlotte said, setting her coffee cup down. "I don't think anyone was fully prepared for how much of a project this acquisition would be. Even

the systems that we deemed compatible in our initial assessment are turning out to be different generations. It's a lot, but thankfully it's still doable, if just barely."

Lisa nodded in understanding. "I think everyone has been caught off guard by the workload this is taking. We knew going into it that it was going to be a lot, but having never been through one of these, I think the leadership still found a way to underestimate it and be overly optimistic."

"Agreed. Luckily, you guys were able to save the day with the data formatting bit. How is that going, by the way?" Charlotte asked.

"It's going well. It was actually going to be one of my discussion points today. My team has developed a proposed plan that I looked at and blessed off on. I wanted you guys to look at it as well, though, and see if there was anything that would conflict with what you were planning. Right now, the plan is to hold everything in temporary systems, let you guys reconfigure the hardware and do what you need to do while we format the data, and then combine it with the new CRM databases. If it all goes according to plan, it should be a fairly seamless transition."

"That makes sense," Charlotte responded. "That's more or less what our initial plan was before we realized we weren't going to have the manning to support that many simultaneous projects. With you guys taking the data piece, though, we should be able to manage it."

"Good. I'll have someone bring the specifics over to you after this meeting. It's a relatively short plan, so it shouldn't take too long to review," Lisa said.

Charlotte smiled in response and took a sip of her coffee while Lisa made her way over to Maria and Will.

"... he's driving everyone crazy," Will was saying in a hushed tone that required Maria to lean in close.

Both glanced up as Lisa approached and Will trailed off his sentence, sharing a glance with Maria before turning and smiling at Lisa.

"Lisa! Good morning."

"Good morning, Will. I hope I'm not interrupting anything important between you two."

"Nonsense," Will said, waving his hand. "We were just talking about office politics. Nothing interesting. I saw you and Charlotte talking. Everything is going well, I assume?"

"As well as can be expected," Lisa replied. "She and I were just discussing the data transformation the security staff took on. After this meeting, she'll have a written proposal for how we want to jointly tackle the problem. I'd love for you to take a look as well."

"Absolutely," Will said. "I'm sure she said it as well, but we do appreciate you guys picking up the slack on that one."

"Just don't make it a habit," Maria said jokingly.

Will threw his head back and laughed out loud, drawing a few confused glances from around the room. "Are you kidding me? But that's our master plan. Eventually we'll have handed off our whole workload to you all and we'll be kicking back on a golf course somewhere, living the dream."

"We'll gladly take over your workload as soon as we can take over your budget as well," Lisa said with a grin.

"Sounds like a deal to me," Will replied. "Just don't come complaining to me when you realize how terrible of a deal that is for you."

Lisa chuckled and walked away from the two of them, making her way to the front of the room. The rest of the people in attendance were slowly breaking apart from their groups and making their way to their seats, a sign that everyone was ready to get this meeting kicked off. Charlotte stood up as Lisa walked by and followed her to the front of the room, the two of them standing there silently as the remaining few stragglers made their way into the room.

"Good morning, everyone," Lisa began. "I hope you all had a good weekend. As all of you are aware, the primary topic today and for the foreseeable future will be the upcoming acquisition. I wouldn't say we're down to the wire yet, but we are certainly getting closer and closer. So far, this partnership between IT and security has done wonders for our productivity, but we are about to be tested. In the next few months, we'll be finalizing the transition and preparing to merge PGF's systems and data with ours. From a security perspective, it's a nightmare. There are a multitude of gaps that we've identified, as well as an unknown number of vulnerabilities that may be created in the process. We'll have to remain vigilant and flexible as we figure it all out. I'll let Charlotte talk the IT piece, but I have no doubt that it's equally as, if not more, daunting as the security concerns."

"We definitely have our hands full," Charlotte said, stepping forward. "I think the best thing we can do right now is identify all the steps we need to take from this moment through completion. At that point, as a group, we can start talking about potential issues that might arise. I'd rather prevent a problem from ever occurring than have to fix it when it blows up in our faces."

With that, Lisa and Charlotte spent the next half hour soliciting input from the room to identify every little step that needed to be taken. The list was longer than even Lisa was expecting, spanning the entirety of two separate whiteboards. Security-specific issues were written in red, IT issues were written in blue, and the joint issues, of which there was a majority, were written in green.

Eventually, everyone in the room agreed that the list was all inclusive. Will proposed they take a ten-minute break to stretch their legs before diving into the analysis and assessment of the list. As everyone filtered out of the room, Will caught both Charlotte and Lisa's eyes and motioned for them to join him and Maria at the table.

"Hey guys, I know we normally like to handle this stuff at our level, but we are about to decide the way ahead for the biggest undertaking our

company has ever done. For this particular decision, I'd like to let Paul and Russell know where we currently are before we go down any rabbit holes. I'd be interested in seeing if they have any input before we go back and forth for the next few hours, coming to an agreement only to have it shot down by either of those two."

"I agree completely," Maria chimed in.

"Makes perfect sense to me," Charlotte said. "I'll go grab Russell."

"I'll get Paul," Lisa replied, making her way to the door.

Before departing, she glanced once more at the two whiteboards standing at the front of the room, trying to decide what she would tell Paul. The list on the boards was extremely daunting, and he would be blindsided walking into the room if he wasn't prepared first. Charlotte was staring at the boards as well, no doubt having reached the same conclusion. Both of them turned towards the door at the same time, sharing a knowing glance with each other as they went to get their bosses.

Chapter 24

Thursday, 27 July

Paul sat quietly in his chair as Brandon carried on. Lisa, sitting next to him, had apparently given up on appearing to pay attention and was instead jotting down a to-do list on a piece of paper. Paul occasionally glanced at it out of the corner of his eye, taking note of what she was writing down. For the most part it appeared to be reminders about upcoming meetings, but towards the bottom she began focusing on the upcoming data formatting they would be doing for the IT department.

Last Monday, after she had come and gotten him, it had been decided that all action would take place in September. The entirety of August would be devoted to planning for it as well as problem-solving issues that could arise. Russell had been fairly easy to work with, agreeing with most points and willing to compromise on those he didn't outright agree with. Of the list that was created on the two whiteboards, they had been able to collectively plan for over eighty percent of it. The remaining items were scheduled to be decided on at the meeting coming Monday.

Brandon was currently going down his own list of items that needed to be done. Paul had already read through the list and noted that there were a handful of references to security concerns. Most of them were benign, and they weren't necessarily what he would have focused on, but at least they were up there. Unlike other weekly meetings, Brandon had actually sent an agenda for this one ahead of time. He wanted to walk through his list of items and then go line by line and have the subject matter expert in the room speak to the proposed solution.

Lisa had quickly written down her thoughts on the security bullets when they entered the room and had handed Paul her notes before beginning to work on her current list. Paul had read over her notes and injected his own thoughts, then set the paper aside and listened to Brandon. While the CEO was a great guy, he was also extremely long-winded and didn't seem to notice when he was losing the audience. Glancing around the

room, Paul could tell that most other people had already tuned Brandon out and were just waiting to be called on so they could answer their piece and move on. Paul wished he were more attentive, but as the minutes dragged on, he found himself equally anxious to just answer his questions and get back to work.

Brandon made a few final comments on how he wanted to prioritize his efforts, with Mitch's efforts being number one as usual, before finally opening it up to the second half of the meeting. The first questions were relative lowballs to Mitch, focusing on his analysis of the markets they were entering as well as a final laydown of the team he would need to support him. Mitch had already answered these questions in previous meetings, so he kept his answers short this time, apparently aware that nobody besides Brandon and Stacy were really paying attention to what he was saying.

Stacy answered her questions next. Hers were a little more pointed, dealing with the current financial status of the company as well as reiterating for the hundredth time that they were still on track to exceed all expectations. Surprisingly, she also brought up current budget requests that her staff was reviewing, noting that the security requests were close to being processed and confirmed. Paul felt an elbow dig into his ribs as Lisa looked up at him, smiling at what Stacy was saying.

Eventually, the questions got around to Russell, who was holding a sheet of paper that Charlotte had handed to him. The first question Brandon had was a general one, asking what the status was regarding preparation for the acquisition. Russell threw a lot of numbers and percentages out as a response, overwhelming everyone in the room with statistics. Brandon attempted to ask a follow-up question relating to one of the statistics, but Russell managed to provide more numbers and avoid providing a direct response. Beside him, Charlotte was writing furiously and attempting to hand Russell a second sheet of paper, which he was pointedly ignoring.

"What about the systems' integration pieces you and I discussed a few weeks ago?" Brandon asked.

"My team is handling it," Russell replied.

Paul couldn't believe what he was hearing. Or rather, he could believe it, he just wasn't thrilled. Russell was pretending his staff was doing everything. He had cleverly made it sound as though his staff was handling the data staging as opposed to the truth, which was that Paul's team had taken over. Lisa was evidently thinking the same thing, because Paul caught her making faces at Charlotte, who looked equally uncomfortable by what was happening. "The biggest problem I see is going to be protecting the data while we format it," Paul interjected. "My team is taking the lead on that in order to make sure it's done properly. Once my team is able to do the full formatting, we should be in a much better place."

Paul glanced across the room and saw Russell glaring at him, clearly having heard Paul's message loud and clear.

"Is that so?" Brandon asked, glancing back and forth between Paul and Russell. "Russell, I thought you said your team was handling it. Are you handing off some tasks to Paul's team?"

"Just the ones that are easy to do," Russell grunted, still glaring at Paul. "His staff wasn't nearly as busy as mine. Besides, he offered to help."

"I think what we're doing for you can hardly be categorized as easy," Lisa said, putting air quotes around the word "easy".

"Personally, I don't care what you think," Russell shot back.

There was a stunned silence in the room as everyone stared awkwardly at either Russell, Paul, Lisa, or Brandon to gauge their reactions.

"Where did that come from?" Paul snapped.

"I'm getting sick and tired of you and your staff trying to be heroes. All of you running around claiming you're protecting us from harm while

overinflating your importance. The fact of the matter is, if need be, my staff could do all the work you're helping us with. I just figured I'd try and make you a part of the team. The joke's on me, I guess."

"Easy, Russell. You, me, and Paul can talk about this later," Brandon said, leaning forward onto the conference table.

"That's bullshit and you know it, Brandon. Everyone here is so enamored with this concept of security," Russel said, practically spitting the word. "Everyone in this room knows how that conversation is going to go."

"That's enough," Brandon reiterated, staring heatedly at Russell. "You and I need to talk about this. Now. Everyone else is free to leave."

"I'll let you know when I have a free moment to talk about all the work you're forcing me to do," Russell snarled, standing up and beating everyone else out the door.

Brandon stood at the head of the table, stunned, watching Russell's back retreat down the hallway. Everyone stood still for a moment, waiting to see if anything would be said, before filtering quietly out of the room to avoid being caught in whatever was going to happen next. Paul remained seated until it was just himself, Stacy, and Brandon in the room.

He opened his mouth to speak but caught Stacy staring at him and shaking her head slightly. Closing his mouth, Paul stood and followed the rest of the staff down the hallway, wondering what the hell had just happened.

Interstitial 3

As noted in the earlier interstitials, communication, a solid foundation, and adherence to the basics is key. So, what communication and what basics did we get in the third section of this book? Was it security- or business-related? The correct answer is: both. What happened was the blending of security with the business needs and the business requirements to achieve a level of communication that's required to maintain the business in this current realm of threats. One of the key things Paul, and more importantly, Mitch did , was bridge a critical gap between the business and security.

From a CFO perspective, the communication, specifically in the form initial ROIs, started to define what the business benefit, impact, and cost of each of these initiatives would be. While not perfect, it's an evolutionary process. IT has had decades to improve on this. Security is still in its formative years. While it has been an inherent part of business for the last few decades, it hasn't reached a plateau point that can be called mature yet.

Yes, we have some incredible tools and there are a great number of providers, vendors, and practitioners that are very mature, but as the technologies evolve and our adversaries evolve more quickly, security is still playing catch-up.

Today, senior executives have a close eye on breaches, ransomware, third-party issues,

Nation State activity, denial of service, data loss, and other highly visible issues that can impact their bottom line. In addition, they are becoming far more concerned with regulatory and industry requirements such as SOX, PCI, HIPAA, and several others that can significantly impact business or land them in jail.

Paul has gone through an iterative process to get to where he is in the third section. He started off as very security-minded but incapable of expanding his viewpoint to the larger business perspective. As he begins to identify this issue, he brings on individuals and works with other executives to create a solution. Throughout the third part, we see him continue this expansion into the non-technical divisions within the company. As he makes his presence, and his responsibilities, better known throughout the company, he is creating a twofold effect. First, he is educating himself so that he can better develop his business plans and present them to the CFO and CEO. Secondly, he is creating an insurgent level of interest in security throughout the company so that it is easier for him to drive the adoption of security measures. A company that understands the why of security is much more likely to enable the proposed solutions.

We have also continued to see the evolution of security awareness from the non-security executives. This is the byproduct of reported security events happening both outside and inside their company. Paul has gotten much

better at defining the risks involved with each of these breaches in a business manner, so that Brandon can easily process the information. Because of this, we have seen Brandon and the board take significant steps in removing roadblocks to Paul's success.

The peer partnering that occurred in the third part of the book portrays elements of common learning with Brandon and Paul, as well as Paul and Mitch. One may argue that Mitch brings more to the table than Paul in the interaction, but the underlying results are really a well-played investment on Mitch's part. With this newfound partnership, the Sales and Services organization has a direct voice in how they perform business and can expect a well-thought-out response and supportive interaction from the security department. This is not an open checkbook for Sales and Services to be able to do anything they want, but the security organization now understands the benefit of supporting the business and can provide more targeted solutions. Additionally, Paul now has the skillset to potentially receive supporting funds for any enhancing or development work or for sustaining resources to ensure that the program is protected and secure.

Creating a message that is business-centric, not fatalistic, provides options and clearly adds ROI. Whether based on clear measurable P&L streams, or somewhat intangible soft dollar results such as risk mitigation, successful security branding can

create a better mechanism for risk/business alignment.

As progressive threats, such as Advanced Persistent Threats (APTs), Ransomware, and other malicious and damaging attacks become prevalent, it's even more important to get the first 90% done. These are basic blocking and tackling items in which partnering with the internal user base (educational), peer support organizations (IT, CTO, DevOps, Big Data, or whatever applicable organizations/resources in your company), and business-facing/-supporting organizations can create a broader, more holistic approach to layering. If done appropriately, a level of empathy, or at least support, is developed.

Paul's relationship with Mitch, Stacy, Brandon, and other key leadership is founded and fostered based on intelligent interaction and trust. Paul is not correct in all instances, nor does the company dodge all malicious attempts. Rather, the framework Paul lays out creates trust based on communication relating to business matters. The security implications he presents are not with a fatalistic viewpoint, but with defined risk/measurements and market analysis to present the case in ROI terms. That alone allows him to drive the business forward in leaps and bounds regarding their security.

PART FOUR

Chapter 25

Monday, 31 July

"You want to do what?" Jerry asked incredulously from across the table.

"I think I was clear. I want to relieve Russell from his role, effective immediately, and promote Charlotte as the interim CIO until we can bring someone in from outside or decide if she is the right candidate to back-fill the position," Brandon replied.

"I think what Jerry was trying to ask was, why do you want to do this? Clearly, there's some impetus for this, considering you called a hasty board meeting to bring this up," Tom said calmly.

"He blatantly disrespected me in front of the rest of the executive leadership. However, besides that, there is a clear track record of him being more of a hindrance than an enabler. He continually acts as though there is only one way of doing things and refuses to see issues from a broader business perspective. I spoke with key members from the security and IT staff yesterday in confidentiality and learned that he has fought back on almost every single security measure the business has tried to put in place. At the end of the day, I feel it is prudent that we remove toxic leadership before we move forward with this acquisition."

"It sounds like you've thought this through," Tom said. "So, tell me, why do you feel that this is a board-level issue?"

"First, I am removing an executive leadership individual that was approved by this board during his hiring. Secondly, I am removing him amid this acquisition, which means we run the risk of disrupting key processes at a critical moment."

"And despite that, you still feel this is the right decision?" Tom asked.

"I do. I have full faith that Charlotte will be able to manage everything. Additionally, I feel that at this point Russell has proven himself more of a liability than an asset. However, before moving forward with this, I wanted to make sure I had the board's full approval."

"Fair enough," Tom replied. "Well then, let's cut to the chase and put it to a vote, shall we? All in favor?"

Brandon looked around the room and noted that all but two hands were raised.

"All opposed?" Tom asked.

The remaining two hands went up while the rest of them went down.

"Very well," Tom said. "You have full board approval to move forward with your plan. However, given that there may be some leadership turbulence, I would ask that you provide the board with periodic updates on all events relating to your IT section. If things start to look poor, I for one would prefer to know sooner rather than later."

"Agreed," Jerry said.

"Additionally," Tom continued, "please make sure we have a PR message for why we are making the leadership changes should anyone ask."

"Too easy," Brandon said. "I'm sure it will be something along the lines of ensuring all of our leadership is readily prepared to take on the complex challenges of a national organization."

"Sounds good to me. Just make sure we don't say anything negative about Russell. I support relieving him of his role, but I absolutely do not support destroying his reputation."

"I completely agree," Brandon said with a nod.

"Alright. Well, now that we've settled that unpleasant issue, is there anything else you'd like to discuss while we are all here in this room together?"

Chapter 26

"There he is! Paul! The man, the myth, the legend, the CIO slayer! Come in, come in!" Mitch shouted as Paul walked towards his office.

Paul cringed, quickly shutting the door behind him.

"You're still calling me that, huh? You know I hate it when you reference Russell as though what happened was my fault," he said, turning to face Mitch.

Mitch laughed, clearly entertained by his own joke. "Oh, you know, I've got to give you some crap for it. Don't get me wrong, nobody I know misses that bastard. Besides, Charlotte is so much more pleasant to work with. I'm just trying to make you out to be the knight in shining armor that everyone needs. Or maybe you're secretly the damsel in distress. I still haven't quite figured it out yet."

"Yeah, yeah, yeah," Paul said, waving his hand dismissively. "Screw you too," he said jokingly.

Mitch laughed again, wiping his eyes as Paul took his seat.

"Hold on one second for me," Mitch finally said. "I've got to send off a quick email to the guy starting the team out at PGF. Now that we're within ninety days of the deadline, we're starting to hammer out some of the details."

"How's that going, by the way?" Paul asked, while Mitch typed up his message.

"It's going well, man. You know what the worst part is? The damn time difference. We planned for everything down to the smallest detail, but no one ever considered that these guys are two hours behind us. It's a real pain in the ass to have to wait until lunch before you get a response.

My wife hates it, because I'll be sitting around after dinner responding to email updates from these guys."

"I'm having the same problem on my end. Luckily, nothing has been time-sensitive yet, but it takes some getting used to. We'll send them a few questions in the morning, knowing that we won't get a response until midafternoon at the earliest," Paul said.

"Same thing here, man," Mitch replied absentmindedly, hitting a few more keys on his keyboard before clicking send and turning to face Paul again. "Sorry about that."

"No worries at all. So, aside from the time difference, how is everything else going?" Paul asked.

"It's all going great. Honestly, I'm super excited for this thing to be finalized so that we can stop planning and start doing. How are things in your area going?"

"Going well. We're swamped with projects right now, but that seems to be the common theme with everyone. Stacy is reviewing my second set of budget requests, but honestly, after all she gave me for my first set of requests, my team is basically set," Paul said.

"That's right!" Mitch said, tapping his forehead. "I forgot to ask about the budget requests. So, they all got approved?"

"Not all of them, but enough of them. And to be honest, that was in large part thanks to you."

"Nah, you're good. Like I said a while ago, you would have gotten there eventually. I just figured I could lend a helping hand. Besides, *you* are the shining example of what this company is all about. I'm just trying to ride your coattails to glory," Mitch said with a wink and a grin.

"I hate you," was all Paul said in response.

Mitch laughed again, leaning back in his chair and letting out a sigh. "Oh man, I'm going to make sure you never live that down."

"I really wish you would."

"Not a chance, man. Anyways, are you guys all set on your end for the next few months? I know things are supposed to be hectic in the IT department in preparation for all this," Mitch said seriously.

"Yeah, we should be fine. We have all the requisite analysis done, and Bill and Maria are currently finalizing the plan for how we're going to merge and integrate all the systems. It'll be busy, but it should work out in the end. To be honest, it's this data formatting thing that's proving to be the pain. It's not overly difficult, but it's taking up more resources than I originally expected."

"That's the thing that caused Russell to lose his mind in that meeting, isn't it?" Mitch asked.

"It is," Paul confirmed.

"It does suck having to spend precious resources helping someone else out. Hopefully, it will all pay off in the long run."

"We'll see about that. I'm not holding my breath, though," Paul said before he really thought about his answer.

"Oh really?" Mitch asked, looking interested.

"Charlotte and her staff are exceptionally busy," Paul said, attempting to backpedal a bit. "I wouldn't feel comfortable asking her to take on any extra work on my behalf. Not until this whole thing is behind us and she's on more even ground."

"Makes sense. I'm not a computer guy, but I can only imagine that taking two individual entities and trying to merge them into one isn't an easy task."

"You have no idea," Paul said, shaking his head.

"Well, anyways, man, is there anything else you wanted to discuss?" Mitch asked, changing gears.

Paul replied, "I figured we hadn't met in a while, so it might be nice to sit down face-to-face and check in. Also, to be candid, there were a few projects and programs Brandon mentioned last month, but I wasn't familiar with them. How can we get ahead of potential issues and pull my organization in earlier so we can be enablers rather than a pain in everyone's ass?"

Mitch thought for a moment before responding, "You know, there are some new projects and initiatives we want to start with our SMB customers. I hadn't really thought about getting your guys involved this early since we are just in ideation."

Mitch paused again in thought. As Paul tried to respond, he continued, "You know, maybe now is the right time to get your team involved. Last year, I was involved in some training for Red Teaming and part of the process was to evaluate things from completely different angles and processes."

Paul was confused. "Red Teams are cybersecurity guys that emulate hackers so we can identify where we have gaps and holes in our systems and processes. How did you go to class for that? You have no technical experience."

Mitch started laughing. "No, they did talk about that, but this was more of a Business Red Teaming process. In fact, I'll lend you the book *Red Teaming* by Bryce Hoffman. Great info that was developed from him working with the U.S. Army. Lots of great tools and thought processes."

"Anyway," Mitch continued, "one of the key items was to get multiple angles and perspectives. What better way to get ahead of things than to have you join early?"

"Perfect, I'll let my staff know and we can start getting the teams involved early on. Is there anything I can do for you?"

"I don't think so. Lisa has been over here this week, evidently coordinating with some of my guys to make some changes to our systems. From the sound of it, whatever you guys are planning on doing should make things easier for us, which I appreciate."

"No worries. That was the goal. We're doing something similar in marketing and HR as well. It costs a little more, but it should help your guys focus on their jobs as opposed to continually having to authenticate themselves."

"Sounds like a winner to me!" Mitch said, smiling. "And it was great to see you again. Sorry it's been so long between meetings recently, but my schedule has been crazy. Things are starting to slow down, though, so feel free to drop by anytime if you have any more questions or just want to vent. I'm sure it's nice to get out of your office occasionally."

"Absolutely. It'll be hectic on my end for the next few weeks, but as soon as we're done with this data transformation issue, I'll be sure to swing back by," Paul said, rising to leave.

Chapter 27

Thursday, 21 September

Taking a deep breath, Paul leaned forward in his chair and began, "Brandon. We've confirmed the issue…"

For the next thirty minutes, he walked Brandon through what he knew, often reiterating information as Brandon, still half asleep, began wrapping his mind around the implications of the breach.

"Do we know who was behind this?" Brandon finally asked.

"All evidence points to this being a combination of an internal person and at least two external actors. Based on log reviews, insider threat activity, and source information our collective teams have compiled with Federal and law enforcement partners, we are extremely confident we have identified them. We will be able to share the identities by the time you get into the office this morning. In the interim, my team is working diligently to ensure there aren't any other issues. We've stopped the breach, so now I'm having them move on to sanitizing the network. I'll keep you apprised of everything that comes up on this end."

"I appreciate it, Paul. Keep up the good work and let me know what you find out. I'll see you in a few hours," Brandon said before ending the call.

Paul sighed and leaned back in his chair, glancing at the clock on the wall and noting it was just after four in the morning. That meant his team had roughly four hours left before the East Coast markets came online and expected everything to be operational. He stood up and stretched his back, grabbing his coffee cup and heading out to refill it.

He stopped by each section of cubicles on the way to the kitchen to check in with the teams and make sure they had all the tools and resources they needed. Everyone assured him they were fine, which was pleasant news all things considered, and by the time Paul was pouring coffee into his mug, he was in a marginally better mood.

"I thought I might catch you here." A voice said over his shoulder.

Paul spun around a bit surprised and found Charlotte standing in the entryway to the kitchen, holding her own empty mug. Paul smiled and held out the coffee pot, filling the mug for her.

"Fancy seeing you here at this hour," he said.

"Word on the street is we got rocked this evening. Care to fill me in?" she asked.

"Sure thing. Let's go to my office," Paul said, walking beside her as they made their way back past all the staff working diligently in front of their computers.

Settling down into the chair behind his desk, Paul slid the papers that Lisa had given them across the desk for Charlotte to read. He nursed his still hot coffee as he watched her absorb all the information without comment.

Finally, having finished the papers, Charlotte set them down on the desk and simply asked, "What can we do to help?"

"Right now, we are in damage control mode. We identified the issue and shut it off as quickly as possible. We are going through everything to make sure there are no more anomalies. As soon as we are done with that, we are going to bring everything back online before the East Coast wakes up. My staff could use all the help they can get with that for now. Once we've handled this issue, I'm going to have my team do a full review of all the ad-hoc things we've done in preparation for this acquisition to make sure we haven't set ourselves up for another problem down the road. I'd appreciate your input on that process as well."

"Sure thing," Charlotte said, nodding. "I'll send some of my teams over here to help go through this for the next few hours. When you're ready, you can hand it back to us, so we can bring everything back online properly. I can only imagine it wasn't taken down properly in the first place, given the haste I'm sure your team was in."

Paul winced and replied, "You're probably right about that."

"It's not an issue at all. At least you were able to stop the problem. I just want to make sure we don't inadvertently cause any more issues."

"Fair enough. I'll let Lisa and Maria know my expectations on the matter. In the meantime, I'm going to start drafting up a situation report to blast out to the rest of the leadership. Anything you care to have mentioned in it?"

"Not yet," Charlotte said. "My team hasn't really done much. I'm sure as we begin digging into this, I'll have comments to make, but for now I'll leave it completely up to you to continue to be the bearer of bad news."

"Thanks for that," Paul said with a chuckle.

"Here for you, buddy," Charlotte responded, grinning as she rose out of her seat to make her way back to her staff.

Paul typed up a quick situation report and sent it to Maria and Lisa, asking them to look over it before he sent it to everyone else. They both responded with approval within minutes, and by 5 a.m., Paul was feeling much more confident with everything that was happening.

At 6:30, his phone rang, displaying the name MITCH on the caller ID. What the hell is he doing at work this early? Paul thought as he reached for the phone.

"Hey Mitch, how's it going?" he answered.

"Probably going better on this end than it is for you," Mitch replied, sounding oddly chipper given the time of morning.

"You're not lying," Paul responded. "How can I help you?"

"I just wanted to shoot you a quick call to figure out what happened. I'm sure my phone will be exploding over this today, and I was wondering if you had a soundbite for me to say to anyone asking."

"Uh, yeah, we are working on that but don't have one yet. Most of the details are in the emails I've been sending out, but the gist of the issue is that we were holding data temporarily in a less than secure environment and that allowed for malicious actors to take advantage of our systems. Some PII was leaked, but as far as we can tell, it wasn't anything catastrophic. We were able to catch it before anything significant was leaked. As I get a more solid grasp on the issue, I'll keep you tied in."

"Appreciate it, bud," Mitch said. "I'm sure you and your team are working their asses off over this. I just know that it's going to be my phone ringing off the hook, and it'll be a nightmare for PR to try and assuage everyone's concerns. Just trying to get out ahead of that."

"I completely understand and will do my best to make sure you have all the answers you need to give to anyone calling," Paul said.

"Sounds good to me," Mitch said, hanging up with a click.

Paul had just placed the phone back on his desk when he heard a knock at his door. Looking up, he saw Lisa standing there with another small stack of papers in her hand.

"Ready for another update?" she asked.

"Sure thing. Come on in," he replied, motioning towards her normal seat.

"We did a complete review and think we've identified who on the inside had a role in this. Unfortunately, it wasn't Russell," she said with a smirk, "but it does look like one of the culprits misused his permissions as an IT admin to pull this off. Charlotte has already been notified and we have already locked that individual's permissions. Her team is already bringing everything back online well in advance of the business requirements. We're confident this was an insider incident, and he was working with two known hackers. The Feds are already on it with the team.. We'll obviously keep our focus on this, but I wanted you to know that we are

officially moving from breach reaction to recovery operations pending your approval."

"Makes perfect sense to me," Paul said.

"Good. Now I'm assuming you'll be sitting down with Brandon later this morning to discuss what happened. I just wanted to give you these," she said, placing the new sheets of paper on the desk. "They're charts to indicate what we currently know, as well as projections for the data we lost and measures of severity for the breach. Additionally, on the last sheet is a list of proposed items that could have potentially stopped this breach. That last sheet is just for you, in case Stacy is there and asks for budgetary considerations."

"Appreciate it," Paul replied, glancing over the papers Lisa had given him.

"No worries at all. Just let me know what else you need from me and my team. I've got a meeting with Will in a few minutes, but I'll be back over here no later than 7 to hopefully give you another update."

Chapter 28

Monday, September 25

"I feel like I'm starting to see a lot more of you than of my own family," Tom said, smiling at everyone around the table. "Now, I'm sure each of you knows why we're here today. Last week, WFG experienced a breach that released some of our customers' personal information. Since then, we have put out multiple PR messages, as well as implemented new security measures, or so I've been told. Brandon here is going to walk us through what we need to know and to discuss any potential lasting implications. Brandon, the floor is yours."

Brandon nodded appreciatively to Tom before clearing his throat and beginning.

"I'm sure each of you has read the report I sent out over the weekend, so I won't insult anyone's intelligence by going into the finite details. In short, we were breached due to internal employees being aware of a security deficiency in some of our data and seeking to capitalize on it. Our cyber security team and law enforcement agencies are taking all appropriate actions.

The best we can tell, is this was all financially motivated. The employee is being dealt with accordingly. As far as who he was working with on the outside, we can't discuss that at this time. What I can say is that it is limited and they are moving forward with arrests. Our security team identified the incident early on and was able to put an end to it before anything truly damaging was released. Mitch and our PR team have been personally reaching out to everyone affected in an attempt to reduce the customer losses we could face. To be completely candid, this could have been much worse. However, Paul and his team were on top of it and were able to prevent anything catastrophic from happening. As it stands now, I firmly believe this was merely a hiccup and should have no effect on the upcoming acquisition."

"I'm hoping you mean the employee is having charges pressed against them when you say they are being dealt with accordingly," Jerry said.

"Our legal team is looking into everything possible. As it stands now, they clearly are guilty of theft and violation of all corporate policies. We may find additional charges as the investigation continues," Brandon replied.

"Do we think we may face any issues of being out of alignment with government-mandated regulations?" Tom asked.

"Our core business was in the best possible alignment with all the regulations. The temporary data that was targeted was admittedly not completely within regulations, but we fixed the problem immediately. As of now, we are planning as though there won't be too large of an issue. Our security posture is stronger now than ever before and Paul is already working diligently on new policies and procedures to put in place."

Tom nodded thoughtfully as he absentmindedly drummed his fingers on the desk.

"I know everyone here is rightfully concerned." Brandon continued. "But I have been talking to Paul and Charlotte continually throughout this entire process and they both have complete confidence that this was an isolated event and should not have any long-term detrimental impact."

"Then I see no reason that this should cause any of us to second-guess our current heading. Does anyone disagree?" Tom asked the group.

After waiting a moment and receiving no reply, he continued, "Very well. Brandon will keep us up to date on all the developments relating to this breach and any future security measures. For the time being, I'm confident in where we are at and feel that this is only a minor speed bump. What's done is done. Let's just work to make sure it doesn't happen again."

Chapter 29

Tuesday, 3 October

As Mitch had suggested to Paul concerning the Red Team, Lisa was now a new member of that business planning review board, evaluating the feasibility of new business objectives.

Jason was new to Mitch's organization and headed up the new review function. He had been a program manager for years and had previously worked for a few security startups. His understanding of security married with the business had started to build bridges. The first idea the teams collaborated on was now a running joke between them.

Over the past few weeks, the security team had been brought in to get early visibility into initiatives the business was evaluating to provide additional services to their customers. At first, the meetings were a bit tense, as the security team shot down everything the business presented due to the potential risks or privacy concerns. Then Jason got involved.

Lisa had been in that first meeting when they reviewed a handful of potential application changes and was appreciative of the new direction the teams had been taking. The request seemed simple: allow their business users the ability to create whatever username they wanted with no character limitations, duplication, or validation checks.

"This seems like an easy one" Jason said.

Lisa spoke up, adding that this may not be as simple as everyone thought. "So, in a company a friend of mine works at, they thought letting the user pick a completely random and unique name just for them would help them remember it better and reduce calls to our help desk. Man, were they wrong!"

She continued, "What they learned was, users are more likely to remember and use their unique email than a unique ID in our system. Not that user-created IDs are bad, but the way they implemented them was just wrong from the start."

"They allowed anything and didn't look for potential duplicates without validation. This meant there could be multiple 'Dave' accounts set up and in collision. It wound up increasing calls to customer service as people forgot their usernames by 45%."

Lisa continued, "Then they had legal issues with highly offensive names with their logo on it. In truth, some were funny, but not conducive to easily working with their products, such as, 'Short woman hiding in tall grass', 'Your mom', or 'I like to eat cheese while riding my bicycle through downtown streets'. Each definitely unique, but not particularly suitable for a business."

The last items had everyone laughing and understanding the need to think through this collaboratively as a group and come up with the best solution to enable the business without shooting themselves in the foot.

Jason smiled back at her. "Thanks for the help in figuring out the best way to that user experience data. I don't think the earlier working team would have had enough experience to know to look where you pointed them to."

Lisa was about to make a lighthearted and sarcastic comment, but instead took a moment and got a bit serious. "I really want to thank you and the team for including us. This has actually been kinda fun! We get to hear about the new business ideas now, so we feel like part of the business, not just a cost center. Normally, we are saying no to the new stuff because you come to us so late." She paused to collect her thoughts.

"The truth is, figuring out new ways to do what you need to do for our customers and stay relevant against our competition has been a new experience. Some of the stuff we have come up with is really cool and should help us be better in all areas."

Jason gave her a soft jab in the shoulder and said, "Gee, you've got me all choked up." Then he gave her a big grin.

"Alright, folks, let's kick this meeting off. We have a long agenda today and we need to make sure we can get the proposal to finance later this week," Jason said as he walked to the whiteboard.

Chapter 30

Stacy looked up from her computer monitor as Paul made his way into her office and took a seat, smiling from ear to ear.

"Happy today?" Stacy asked, arching an eyebrow.

"I'm always happy when I get to come talk with you," Paul said with a wink.

"How charming," Stacy laughed. "Speaking of charming, I'm assuming you did something to make the whole anniversary debacle up to your wife?"

"Oh yeah. We went out to a nice dinner and a play this past weekend. For some reason, the breach excuse didn't hold much weight when it came to explaining to her why I wasn't there for the actual day."

"I can't imagine why," Stacy said, dramatically rolling her eyes.

Paul laughed in response and leaned back slightly in his chair, taking on a much more comfortable posture.

"So, what can I do for you?" he asked.

"I got your post-breach emergency purchase requests," Stacy said, pointing at her computer monitor. "I just wanted to say that they all make perfect sense and Brandon should have no issues with all of these being funded immediately."

"You wanted me to stop by to tell me you don't need anything else from me?" Paul asked.

"I suppose I could have done it via email, but I wanted to talk with you in person. Paul, these requests are exactly in line with what my team is looking for. I just wanted to show you a side-by-side of one of your first

budget requests compared to the ones you submitted last week. The difference is night and day."

"I appreciate that," Paul said, leaning forward and looking at the examples she had pulled up on her computer. "I may not be the smartest guy in the room, but at least I can follow directions, right?"

Stacy rolled her eyes again in response.

"Fair enough," Paul said with a smile. "Is there anything else I can do for you, though? Surely, you didn't want to just sit me down and tell me the good news and then have me leave."

"Actually, there is one other thing. A couple of individuals in the other business units have continued to have issues with validating their budget requests. I know Mitch took you under his wing and helped mentor you to this point. I was wondering if you'd be willing to pay it forward and help some other key individuals who are still struggling."

"Absolutely," Paul said, a look of seriousness overtaking his face as he leaned forward in his chair. "Just tell me who."

EPILOGUE

While these characters and this story are fictional, the featured challenges and processes are tried and proven. Some events and scenarios even share extreme similarities to real-world incidents.

The ideas represented in this book are not a fool-proof method. There will be many iterations, attempts, and trials to successfully position the perception and trust in a business, both interdepartmentally and among the executive staff. Expect that with new threats, evolving metrics, and KPIs, as well as changed perception, there will be constant changes to the message being presented.

The main takeaway? Timing is everything. In many instances, it has taken years for security professionals to gain the visibility and funding to progress specific security programs. Could they have been done earlier for less money and with better results? Probably. Did they fit the current business focus? No. While they were forward-thinking and could have resulted in a slightly higher ROI, the timing and risk posture of the business meant that the program(s) was not funded.

The ideal situation is to have the plans in place and ready to be leveraged when necessary. There will be breaches. There will be active threats. "Never waste a good breach." Always have a handy list to refer to so you can react rapidly and gain additional funding.

The plan doesn't have to be 100% accurate, nor does it have to be overly detailed. But you do need plans and strategic vision to ensure you can capitalize quickly on a negative event.

There is no magic in securing a business.

- It is hard work.
- It is thankless work, most of the time.
- It is about understanding the business you are trying to secure.
- It is about basics.

- It is about communication.
- It is about security training; all resources, not just the security team.

Most of all – it is about the people and leadership that ensure it happens well, every time.

Make no mistake: no matter how well a business prepares, no matter how many measures a company has in place, no matter the tools or resources invested in, every business is a target. Most already have been compromised; many just don't realize it.

This statement is not meant to deter executives from doing what needs to be done, nor is it full of doom and gloom. It is about understanding the current situation. Knowing this enables businesses to be prepared, respond appropriately, and take realistic approaches to their security model.

From large-scale breaches and data loss to denial-of-service attacks, companies are resilient. Most of the companies you've read about in the news have recovered from breaches and losses, even though their names are now synonymous with specific breach and fraud types in the security industry. The hope of all companies is not to be featured on the front pages of newspapers due to a security event. However, the sad reality is that as basics are ignored or not followed, and as better breach/hack methodologies and vectors arise, chances are that a company *will* eventually face a breach. Therefore, not the breach itself, but the action plan on how to react and respond is key to staying out of the newspapers, as are the lessons learned that should ultimately drive continual improvement and prevention.

Plan. Execute. Reassess. Repeat.

There are multiple vulnerability points and vectors that are at risk or allow breaches/hacks to occur. A common and recommended approach is to create security in a layered and pragmatic approach. Commonly referred to as Defense in Depth (DiD), this approach considers any

individual layer that can be vulnerable and breached/bypassed and has secondary/tertiary layers at each vulnerable layer. By defining security in this manner, security leaders and senior business executives can create a targeted approach that can be measured and conducted with relatively low-cost methods and procedures.

For the non-security professional, imagine Defense in Depth as a medieval city with a castle at its center. Numerous elements of DiD can be exemplified with the castle/keep imagery.

Most medieval towns/cities were designed to be defensive in nature and protect the inhabitants against invaders:

- The majority were built on high ground so they could take advantage of a clear field of vision. Consider this your cyber visibility and threat awareness.
- They may have had natural barriers, such as large bodies of water, mountain ranges, or other difficult traversal areas. These are foundational and could be as simple as disabling unused protocols or consistent patch methodologies.
- Walls and moats were built to protect and fortify. These are like firewalls, anti-virus software, endpoint protection, and other blocking mechanisms.
- Choke points, obstructed entry ways, and guards were common entry points. This can be synonymous to Identity and Access Management, least privilege, parts of Zero Trust.
- To be somewhat confusing to those not from the keep, there were very few straight and narrow streets or avenues that allowed invaders to easily navigate the environment. While I'm not a proponent of Security by Obfuscation, I am in favor of limiting blast radius and not directly/openly connecting disparate systems or services.
- As the defenders withdrew from an attack, there were choke points and areas that allowed for easier defense of the town; the

defense became focused and harder to breach. This is the Zero Trust concept and the idea of defense at each asset.

- All the town inhabitants (typically serfs) picked up whatever weapon they could, whether pitchfork or carving knife, and defended the castle inside the inner walls. Again, this is where cybersecurity is no different. Everyone has a role to play, large or small.
- As proactive measures, most had spies, informants, or other ways of getting information. Threat intelligence is a critical starting point to ensure you know what to protect, from whom, and how.

All these are corollaries to cybersecurity. This is not a complete list, but you can see how there is a simple mapping from the physical world to cyber.

No single element is enough to protect your business. Advance thought and planning needs to be employed to ensure that gaps are covered. Everyone has a role and responsibility, regardless of position or capabilities.

At the heart of this is *not* having "security as an afterthought" and instead moving security earlier in the planning as a key element to consider with every business action. This is a pairing of business needs and basic security concepts. Security as an afterthought is far more expensive and time-consuming, as you need to modify and protect the noted layers. Again, this planning and thought process does NOT require or demand that all the tooling, capabilities, and cost be created and deployed up front. Instead, it only means these elements need to be considered and you need to have an associated roadmap to ensure that when time, funding, and resources are available, they are included into the operational security toolbox.

Don't get so caught up by what you don't have that you start experiencing analysis paralysis. Instead, start with the basics. Evaluate what needs to

be done. Execute. It won't be perfect. It won't ever be finished. But it is a foundation you can build on daily.

Within every industry, every company, and every business unit, there are key decisions to be made at the most basic level – Return on Investment. No business organization has ever said, "We have more than enough funds to work on every project and program that we want to work on, and regardless of the cost, we will do what we want." Every decision in every business is based on the cost versus the potential earned and/or saved. This is the absolute point that every security professional needs to understand. While there are critical defensive items you need to put in place to protect your business, they cannot all be done. Even if the funding and resources were available, time is always a constraint. This means that the security leadership needs to create a viable and realistic roadmap of layered protective measures. People (insourced or outsourced), technology, processes, unique threats to your market sector, etc. all need to be considered when creating the roadmap and the overview that senior executives require to determine who gets a slice of the proverbial funding pie.

A well-thought-out and formulated plan that clearly articulates the drivers, expenses, and measurable components creates a more affordable and marketable plan when presenting to those within the company that make the funding decisions.

Stay abreast of current issues. This is as true for the security leadership as it is for the other executive staff. While the security leaders should be the core knowledge base, a common and basic understanding of implications in each given industry is key. As executives are held accountable for corporate direction and actions, well-informed decisions are paramount. One item that has had success in many industries is well-staged tabletop exercises or war games. These involve many areas of the business and can act as training exercises, validation of M&Ps, and interactive communication points and stimulate questions from all participants.

It is every leader's role to understand security implications. It is every *security* leader's role to understand the Governance, Risk, Compliance components, plan for mitigation that is realistic for the business they protect and communicate that in a way that allows business leaders to make the best decisions possible based on the provided information.

At the end of the day, leading an effective security organization is as much about understanding the business, as it is about understanding the technical aspect of security. Whether you are the CISO leading the entire organization, or a manager focused on a specific part, this is key to developing a realistic and sufficient security system for your business.